FINDING
JOY IN
EVERY
MOMENT

# "Nothing is worth more than this day."

## Kathryn & Ross Petras

Workman Publishing · New York

Library of Congress Cataloging-in-Publication Data is available.

ISBN 978-0-7611-8608-3

Design by Vaughn Andrews

Workman books are available at special discounts when purchased in bulk
for premiums and sales promotions as well as for fund-raising or educational
use. Special editions or book excerpts can also be created to specification. For
details, contact the Special Sales Director at the address below, or send an
email to specialmarkets@workman.com.

Workman Publishing Company, Inc.
225 Varick Street
New York, NY 10014-4381

workman.com

WORKMAN is a registered trademark of Workman Publishing Co., Inc.

Printed in the United States of America
First printing March 2016

10 9 8 7 6 5 4 3

## INTRODUCTION

"There is always something to celebrate, whether it is the first green tip of a snowdrop pushing up or the gathering of suncrisped shirts fresh off the clothesline. There are flowers to count and fruit to harvest." So said artist Nikki McClure.

And she is right. There is always something to celebrate . . . which is the point of this book. We've collected 337 quotations to remind us all that if you know where and how to look, you'll always find something to make you smile, to give you a shot of positive energy, and to allow you to rejoice in life.

*Nothing Is Worth More Than This Day* is a pick-me-up for those days when you just want to crawl back into bed and pull the covers over your head. It's also a call to action—a means for getting and maintaining a positive attitude (which may even make you richer, at least according to research by psychologist Suzanne Segerstrom, who found that optimistic law students earned an average of $32,667 more than their pessimistic peers!). But happiness is its own reward, of course, as the people quoted in this book—from Roman emperors to jazz musicians, from Maya Angelou to Frank Zappa—would quickly tell you. It's a varied group, but they have one thing in common: They know how to find happiness no matter what.

Ultimately, much boils down to how you choose to look at things. For example, take the old "Is the glass half empty or half full?" question. Optimists, it is said, see that proverbial glass as half full, while pessimists see it as half empty. But others point out that the glass is actually completely full—half with water and the other half with air. And still others say, "Who cares?"—all you have to do is get a pitcher of water and fill the dang glass!

And that's exactly what this book is designed to do—to fill your proverbial glass with optimism and good cheer, with quotes from people who embrace the day and celebrate life in all of its fullness.

# The beginning is always today.

—attributed to
MARY WOLLSTONECRAFT, *feminist/writer*

#2
.....

My future starts when I wake up every morning. That's when it starts—when I wake up and see the first light. Then, I'm grateful.

—**MILES DAVIS**, *jazz musician*

# 3
·····

Every day we are engaged in a miracle which we don't even recognize: a blue sky, white clouds, green leaves, the black, curious eyes of a child—our own two eyes. All is a miracle.

—Thích Nhất Hạnh, *Buddhist monk*

# 4
.....

People don't
realize, how
important it
is to wake up
every morning
with a song in
your heart.

—JIDDU KRISHNAMURTI, *philosopher*

# 5

It takes no more time to see the good side of life than to see the bad.

—JIMMY BUFFETT, *singer/songwriter*

**#6**
.....

"What day is it?"
"It's today,"
squeaked Piglet.
"My favorite day,"
said Pooh.

—A. A. MILNE, *writer*

**#7**
· · · · ·

# Rules for Happiness: something to do, someone to love, something to hope for.

—IMMANUEL KANT, *philosopher*

#8
•••••

If you feel like tapping your feet, tap your feet. If you feel like clapping your hands, clap your hands. And if you feel like taking off your shoes, take off your shoes. We are here to have a ball. So we want you to leave your worldly troubles outside and come in here and swing.

—ART BLAKEY, *jazz musician*

**#9**

You can't deny laughter; when it comes, it plops down in your favorite chair and stays as long as it wants.

—STEPHEN KING, *writer*

*#10*

I have found
that if you
love life,
life will love
you back.

—ARTHUR RUBINSTEIN, *classical pianist*

*# 11*
......

At times our own
light goes out and is
rekindled by a spark
from another person.
Each of us has cause
to think with deep
gratitude of those
who have lighted the
flame within us.

—ALBERT SCHWEITZER, *humanitarian*

*#12*

# Stay low, stay quiet, keep it simple, don't expect too much, enjoy what you have.

—DEAN KOONTZ, *writer*

# #13
......

If the only prayer you said in your whole life was "Thank You," that would suffice.

—MEISTER ECKHART, *theologian/philosopher*

**#14**

# When you arise in the morning, think of what a precious privilege it is to be alive— to breathe, to think, to enjoy, to love.

—MARCUS AURELIUS, *emperor/philosopher*

# 15
••••••

One of the
secrets of a
happy life is
continuous
small treats.

—Iris Murdoch, *writer*

*#16*
·······

Since you get more
joy out of giving
joy to others, you
should put a good
deal of thought
into the happiness
that you are able
to give.

—ELEANOR ROOSEVELT, *humanitarian*

**# 17**

If everyone
started off
the day singing,
just think
how happy
they'd be.

—LAUREN MYRACLE, *writer*

**#18**
·······

# If it sounds good and feels good, then it *is* good!

—DUKE ELLINGTON, *jazz musician*

# #19

Your problem is how you are going to spend this one odd and precious life you have been issued. Whether you're going to live it trying to look good and creating the illusion that you have power over people and circumstances, or whether you are going to taste it, enjoy it, and find out the truth about who you are.

—**ANNE LAMOTT,** *writer*

*#20*

# Life isn't about waiting for the storm to pass...it's about learning to dance in the rain.

—VIVIAN GREENE, *writer*

*# 21*
.......

# The more you praise and celebrate your life, the more there is in life to celebrate.

—OPRAH WINFREY, *media mogul*

## # 22

These flowers will be rotten in a couple hours. Birds will crap on them. The smoke here will make them stink, and tomorrow a bulldozer will probably run over them, but for right now they are so beautiful.

—CHUCK PALAHNIUK, *writer*

**#26**
.......

I, not events, have the
power to make me happy
or unhappy today. I can
choose which it shall
be. Yesterday is dead,
tomorrow hasn't arrived
yet. I have just one day,
today, and I'm going
to be happy in it.

—GROUCHO MARX, *comedian/producer*

# Stop a moment, cease your work, look around you.

—LEO TOLSTOY, *writer*

**#24**

I can't begin to describe a day as wonderful as this. One marvel after another, each lasting less than five minutes, it was enough to drive one mad.

—CLAUDE MONET, *painter*

# 23

With the Past as past I have nothing to do, nor with the Future as future. I live now, & will verify (the) all past history in my own moments.

—RALPH WALDO EMERSON, *poet/essayist*

# 27
......

# Each day, in itself, brings with it an eternity.

—PAULO COELHO, *writer*

#28

# If you enjoy living, it is not difficult to keep the sense of wonder.

—RAY BRADBURY, *writer*

*#29*

If we are ever to enjoy life, now is the time—not tomorrow, nor next year, nor in some future life after we have died. . . . Today should always be our most wonderful day.

—**THOMAS DREIER**, *editor/business theorist*

#30

# Laughter is an instant vacation.

—MILTON BERLE, *comedian*

*# 31*

It doesn't matter if I'm off the beat. It doesn't matter if I'm snapping to the rhythm. It doesn't matter if I look like a complete goon when I dance. It is my dance. It is my moment. It is mine. And dance I will. Try and stop me. You'll probably get kicked in the face.

—DAN PEARCE, *writer*

# I'm just enjoying my life. I suggest you try it.

—TYLER PERRY, *actor/director*

# #33

You will never be happy if you continue to search for what happiness consists of. You will never live if you are looking for the meaning of life.

—ALBERT CAMUS, *writer*

# # 34

Let a joy keep you.
Reach out your
   hands
And take it when it
   runs by.

—CARL SANDBURG, *poet*

*# 38*

# When reality looks too ugly, fantasize.

—JIMMY BUFFETT, *singer/songwriter*

# 37

# It is fun to have fun But you have to know how.

—DR. SEUSS, *writer/illustrator*

# *36*

One of the most tragic things I know about human nature is that all of us tend to put off living. We are all dreaming of some magical rose garden over the horizon—instead of enjoying the roses that are blooming outside our windows today.

—DALE CARNEGIE, *writer/lecturer*

# 35
·······

Pick the day. Enjoy it—to the hilt. The day as it comes. People as they come. . . . The past, I think, has helped me appreciate the present—and I don't want to spoil any of it by fretting about the future.

—AUDREY HEPBURN, *actress/humanitarian*

**# 39**

I think it's a cool thing to just wake up and write. It was beautiful earlier today—the sky was outrageous. Rembrandt, Picasso, van Gogh, they don't have a palette like that. That firmament that God gets to work with every day, even on a lazy day, just blows your mind.

—**WOODY HARRELSON**, *actor*

# 40

Life is short and there will always be dirty dishes, so let's dance.

—JAMES HOWE, *writer*

**# 41**

Happy. Just in my swim shorts, barefooted, wild-haired, in the red fire dark, singing, swigging wine, spitting, jumping, running—that's the way to live.

—JACK KEROUAC, *writer*

*# 42*
.......

I'm struck by how laughter connects you with people. It's almost impossible to maintain any kind of distance or any sense of social hierarchy when you're just howling with laughter. Laughter is a force for democracy.

—JOHN CLEESE, *actor/writer*

# 43

There it is—happiness. Here it comes, closer and closer. I can hear its footsteps. And if *we* never see it or know it, well, that's all right too. Others will.

—ANTON CHEKHOV, *writer*

NOTHING IS WORTH MORE...

**# 44**

As long as I live, I'll hear
waterfalls and birds and
winds sing. I'll interpret
the rocks, learn the
language of flood, storm,
and the avalanche. I'll
acquaint myself with the
glaciers and wild gardens,
and get as near the heart
of the world as I can.

—JOHN MUIR, *naturalist*

Life's a sh*t sandwich, my ass. Life's a polka and don't you forget it!

—WALLY LAMB, *writer*

# 46

I have not yet lost the
feeling of wonder, and
of delight, that this
delicate motion should
reside in all the ordinary
things around us,
revealing itself only to
him who looks for it.
I remember, in the winter
of our first experiments,
just seven years ago,

looking on snow with new eyes. There the snow lay around my doorstep—great heaps of protons quietly precessing in the earth's magnetic field. To see the world for a moment as something rich and strange is the private reward of many a discovery.

—EDWARD M. PURCELL, *physicist*

# 47

# Either peace or happiness, let it enfold you.

—CHARLES BUKOWSKI, *writer*

**#48**

Laughter is
immeasurable.
Be joyful
though you
have considered
all the facts.

—WENDELL BERRY,
*environmental activist/writer*

# *49*

# As long as we live, there is never enough singing.

—**MARTIN LUTHER,** *religious leader*

**# 50**

And I learned what is obvious to a child. That life is simply a collection of little lives, each lived one day at a time. That each day should be spent finding beauty in flowers and poetry and talking to animals. That a day spent with dreaming and sunsets and refreshing breezes cannot be bettered.

—**NICHOLAS SPARKS,** *writer*

## # 51

If the sight of the blue skies fills you with joy, if a blade of grass springing up in the fields has power to move you, if the simple things of nature have a message that you understand, rejoice, for your soul is alive.

—ELEONORA DUSE, *actress*

# 52

God has blessed you richly, so get down on your knees and thank him. Don't forget the less fortunate or God will personally kick your ass. I'd love to do it for him, but I can't be everywhere.

—**Willie Nelson**, *singer/songwriter*

**#53**

# Dance till the stars come down with the rafters Dance, dance, dance till you drop.

—W. H. AUDEN, *poet*

# 54

Neglect no opportunity to play leap-frog. It is the best of all games and will never become professionalized.

—P. G. WODEHOUSE, *humorist*

*# 55*
• • • • • •

# Think big thoughts, but relish small pleasures.

—H. JACKSON BROWN JR., *writer*

# 56

Can you see the holiness in those things you take for granted—a paved road or a washing machine? If you concentrate on finding what is good in every situation, you will discover that your life will suddenly be filled with gratitude, a feeling that nurtures the soul.

—HAROLD KUSHNER, *rabbi/writer*

# 57

Everything in the world is beautiful, but Man only recognizes beauty if he sees it either seldom or from afar. . . . Listen, today we are gods! Our blue shadows are enormous. We move in a gigantic, joyous world.

—VLADIMIR NABOKOV, *writer*

# 58

To me, life without veal stock, pork fat, sausage, organ meat, demi-glace, or even stinky cheese is a life not worth living.

—ANTHONY BOURDAIN, *chef/writer*

*# 59*
.......

# If you look the right way, you can see that the whole world is a garden.

—FRANCES HODGSON BURNETT, *writer*

**# 60**

What I know for sure is that every day brings a chance for you to draw in a breath, kick off your shoes, and step out and dance—to live free of regret and filled with as much joy, fun, and laughter as you can stand.

—OPRAH WINFREY, *media mogul*

# 61
·······

...joy in
an old
pencil is
not absurd.

—MAY SARTON, *writer*

**# 62**

We can't actually fly to another planet. But we can recapture that sense of having just tumbled out to life on a new world by looking at our own world in unfamiliar ways.

—RICHARD DAWKINS, *scientist*

**#63**

All this he saw, for one moment breathless and intense, vivid on the morning sky; and still, as he looked, he lived; and still, as he lived, he wondered.

—**KENNETH GRAHAME,** *writer*

**# 64**

Tell the truth.
Sing with passion.
Work with
laughter.
Love with heart.
'Cause that's
all that matters
in the end.

—KRIS KRISTOFFERSON, *singer/songwriter*

# 65

Why aren't you dancing with joy at this very moment? is the only relevant spiritual question.

—VILAYAT INAYAT KHAN, *spiritual leader*

# 66
·······

# Be happy. It's one way of being wise.

—COLETTE, *writer*

*# 67*

# Isn't it nice to think that tomorrow is a new day with no mistakes in it yet?

—L. M. MONTGOMERY, *writer*

# 68

The things that brought me the most comfort now were too small to list. Raspberries in cream. Sparrows with cocked heads. Shadows of bare limbs making for sidewalk filigrees. Roses past their prime with their petals loose about them. The shouts of children at play in the neighborhood, Ginger Rogers on the black-and-white screen.

—**ELIZABETH BERG**, *nurse/writer*

*# 69*

When you do something noble and beautiful and nobody noticed, do not be sad. For the sun every morning is a beautiful spectacle and yet most of the audience still sleeps.

—**JOHN LENNON,** *musician/songwriter*

# 70

For one wild, glad moment we snapped the chain that binds us to earth, and joining hands with the winds we felt ourselves divine!

—HELEN KELLER, *humanitarian/writer*

# 71
.......

Make
connections;
let rip;
and dance
whenever
you can.

—ANNIE DILLARD, *writer*

# 72

# Pie makes everybody happy.

—LAURIE HALSE ANDERSON, *writer*

# #73
·······

Just now, I press the elevator
button and am thankful that
it arrives quickly.

I get onto the elevator and
am thankful that the elevator
cable didn't snap and plummet
me to the basement.

I go to the fifth floor and am
thankful that I didn't have to
stop on the second or third or
fourth floor.

I get out and am thankful that
Julie left the door unlocked so
I don't have to rummage for my
King Kong key ring.

I walk in, and am thankful that Jasper is home and healthy and stuffing his face with pineapple wedges.

And on and on. I'm actually muttering to myself, "Thank you . . . thank you . . . thank you."

It's an odd way to live. But also kind of great and powerful. I've never before been so aware of the thousands of little good things, the thousands of things that go right every day.

—A. J. JACOBS, *writer*

# 74
. . . . . . .

He is a wise man who does not grieve for the things he has not, but rejoices for those which he has.

—EPICTETUS, *philosopher*

**# 75**

Thank goodness for the first snow, it was a reminder—no matter how old you became and how much you'd seen, things could still be new if you were willing to believe they still mattered.

—CANDACE BUSHNELL, *columnist/writer*

**# 76**

# Think of all the beauty that's still left in and around you and be happy.

—**ANNE FRANK**, *diarist*

**# 77**

# As long as there was coffee in the world, how bad could things be?

—CASSANDRA CLARE, *writer*

*# 78*

On with the dance, let joy be unconfined is my motto, whether there's any dance to dance, or any joy to unconfine.

—**MARK TWAIN**, *humorist*

# # 79

# The world is full of magic things, patiently waiting for our senses to grow sharper.

—W. B. YEATS, *poet*

*# 80*

Consider the lilies of the field. Look at the fuzz on a baby's ear. Read in the backyard with the sun on your face. Learn to be happy. And think of life as a terminal illness, because, if you do, you will live it with joy and passion, as it ought to be lived.

—ANNA QUINDLEN, *writer*

*# 81*
• • • • • •

# I don't trust anyone who doesn't laugh.

—MAYA ANGELOU, *writer*

*# 82*

# My mom used to say, "a truly happy person is one who can enjoy the scenery on a detour."

—GREGORY BENFORD, *astrophysicist/writer*

# # 83

A homeless man visited my store today. The few quarters that he had in his pocket he invested on books. I offered him free books, but he insisted on giving me his quarters. He walked away filled with joy as if he possessed the world's riches in his hands. In a way, he did. He left me smiling and knowing that he was wealthier than many others.

—BESA KOSOVA, *literacy advocate/poet*

**# 84**

# The present moment is filled with joy and happiness. If you are attentive, you will see it.

—THÍCH NHẤT HẠNH, *Buddhist monk*

*# 85*

# Live in the sunshine, swim the sea, drink the wild air's salubrity.

—RALPH WALDO EMERSON, *poet/essayist*

# Nothing is worth more than this day.

—JOHANN WOLFGANG VON GOETHE,
*writer*

*# 87*

# There is not one blade of grass, there is no color in this world that is not intended to make us rejoice.

—JOHN CALVIN, *religious leader*

## # 88

I am grateful for
what I am & have. My
thanksgiving is perpetual.
It is surprising how
contented one can be
with nothing definite—
only a sense of existence.
Well anything for variety.
I am ready to try this for
the next 1000 years, &
exhaust it. How sweet to
think of! My extremities

well charred, and my intellectual part too, so that there is no danger of worm or rot for a long while. My breath is sweet to me. O how I laugh when I think of my vague indefinite riches. No run on my bank can drain it—for my wealth is not possession but enjoyment.

—HENRY DAVID THOREAU, *naturalist/writer*

**#89**

You are imperfect,
permanently and
inevitably flawed.
And you are
beautiful.

—AMY BLOOM, *writer*

# 90

I find ecstasy in living—the mere sense of living is joy enough.

—EMILY DICKINSON, *poet*

# 91

Joy does not simply happen to us. We have to choose joy and keep choosing it every day.

—Henri J. M. Nouwen, *priest/humanitarian*

**# 92**

Breath and life, and the opportunity to try. If you have nothing more, you always have that.

—ALICIA KEYS, *musician/songwriter*

# #93

You think this is
just another day in
your life? It's not just
another day. It's the
one day that is given to
you today. It's given to
you. It's a gift. It's the
only gift that you have
right now, and the only
appropriate response
is gratefulness. If you

do nothing else but to cultivate that response to the great gift that this unique day is, if you learn to respond as if it were the first day in your life and the very last day, then you will have spent this day very well.

—LOUIE SCHWARTZBERG, *filmmaker*

I look out the window
and I see the lights and
the skyline and the
people on the street
rushing around looking
for action, love, and the
world's greatest chocolate
chip cookie, and my
heart does a little dance.

—NORA EPHRON, *writer/journalist*

**# 95**

Self-actualizing people have the wonderful capacity to appreciate again and again, freshly and naïvely, the basic goods of life, with awe, pleasure, wonder, and even ecstasy.

—A. H. MASLOW, *psychologist*

*# 96*
·······

# Don't look at your feet to see if you are doing it right. Just dance.

—**ANNE LAMOTT,** *writer*

*# 97*
•••••••

# Enthuse, widely and often.

—CHRISTINE WONG YAP, *artist*

# # 98

As long as the sun's shining, sh\*t can't be that bad.

—J. LYNN, *writer*

**# 99**

Sometimes it's moments like that, real complicated moments, absorbing moments, that make you realize that even hard times have things in them that make you feel alive. And then there's music, and girls, and drugs, and homeless people who've read Pauline Kael, and wah-wah pedals, and English potato chip flavors, and I haven't even read *Martin Chuzzlewit* yet. . . . There's plenty out there.

—**NICK HORNBY,** *writer*

**#100**

I was especially perceptive to all things beautiful that morning— raspberries in blue china bowls were enough to make the heart sing.

—IRENE HUNT, *writer*

**#101**

Live in each season as it passes; breathe the air, drink the drink, taste the fruit, and resign yourself to the influences of each.

—HENRY DAVID THOREAU, *naturalist/writer*

# *#102*

Seize the moments of happiness, love and be loved! That is the only reality in the world, all else is folly. It is the one thing we are interested in here.

—LEO TOLSTOY, *writer*

**#103**

# A table, a chair, a bowl of fruit and a violin; what else does a man need to be happy?

—ALBERT EINSTEIN, *physicist*

It was only a
sunny smile, and
little it cost in the
giving, but like
morning light
it scattered the
night and made
the day worth
living.

—F. SCOTT FITZGERALD, *writer*

# *#105*

# Rosiness is not a worse windowpane than gloomy gray when viewing the world.

—**GRACE PALEY,** *writer/activist*

**#106**

you are a
universe
of universes
and your
soul a source
of songs.

—RUBÉN DARÍO, *poet*

**#107**

# Everything in the universe has a rhythm. Everything dances.

—MAYA ANGELOU, *writer*

## #108

For most of life, nothing wonderful happens. If you don't enjoy getting up and working and finishing your work and sitting down to a meal with family or friends, then the chances are you're not going to be very happy. If someone bases his happiness or unhappiness on major events like a great job, huge amounts of money, a flawlessly happy marriage, or a trip to Paris, that person isn't going to be happy much of the time. If, on the other hand, happiness depends on a good breakfast, flowers in the yard, a drink or a nap, then we are more likely to live with quite a bit of happiness.

—**ANDY ROONEY,** *journalist/news commentator*

**#109**
••••••••

# Nobody can be uncheered with a balloon.

—A. A. MILNE, *writer*

# # 110

When, on a moonlit night,
you see a wide village street
with its peasant houses,
haystacks, sleeping willows,
tranquility enters the soul; in
this calm, wrapped in the shade
of night, free from struggle,
anxiety and passion, everything
is gentle, wistful, beautiful,
and it seems that the stars
are watching over it tenderly
and with love, and that this
is taking place somewhere
unearthly, and that all is well.

—ANTON CHEKHOV, *writer*

*# 111*

We are all here
for a spell, get
all the good
laughs you can.

—**WILL ROGERS,** *writer*

# # 112

In the joy of your heart may you feel the living joy that sang one spring morning, sending its glad voice across a hundred years.

—RABINDRANATH TAGORE, *writer*

**#113**

The trick is to enjoy
life. Don't wish away
your days, waiting
for better ones ahead.
The grand and the
simple. They are
equally wonderful.

—**MARJORIE PAY HINCKLEY,** *writer*

**# 114**

Rejoice in
the things
that are
present;
all else is
beyond thee.

—MICHEL EYQUEM DE MONTAIGNE, *essayist*

**# 115**

I got the blues thinking of the future, so I left off and made some marmalade. It's amazing how it cheers one up to shred oranges and scrub floors.

—D. H. LAWRENCE, *writer*

# 116

Every day is
a gift—a new
beginning . . .
bound out
of bed with
the enthusiasm
of a child.

—JOYE MOON, *artist*

Years ago I had a
Buddhist teacher
in Thailand who
would remind all his
students that there
was always something
to be thankful for.
He'd say, "Let's rise
and be thankful, for
if we didn't learn a

lot today, at least we may have learned a little. And if we didn't learn even a little, at least we didn't get sick. And if we did get sick, at least we didn't die. So let us all be thankful."

—LEO BUSCAGLIA, *professor/writer*

# *# 118*

I yelled for joy.
We passed the bottle.
The great blazing
stars came out, the
far-receding sand hills
got dim. I felt like
an arrow that could
shoot out all the way.

—JACK KEROUAC, *writer*

*# 119*

# Joy is the grace we say to God.

—RAY BRADBURY, *writer*

*# 120*
........

You're not going
to make me have
a bad day. If there's
oxygen on earth
and I'm breathing,
it's going to be
a good day.

—COTTON FITZSIMMONS,
*basketball coach*

# 121

The spectacle
of the sky
overwhelms me.
I'm overwhelmed
when I see a
crescent moon
or the sun in an
immense sky.

—JOAN MIRÓ, *artist*

# Life is more fun if you play games.

—ROALD DAHL, *writer*

# #123

Oh, the country! *Ahhhh.* . . .
The fresh, breezy meadow
out back. The air just
galumphs toward you.
It sweeps and sweeps and
sweeps and sweeps over you
and you go, *Ahhhh.* And the
meadowlarks singing! That's
what I'd wake up to every
morning in Iowa. *Ahhhh.*
But I sure hated the flies
and the mosquitoes.

—CLORIS LEACHMAN, *actress*

*# 124*

# We don't know where we're going, but isn't it fun to go?

—L. M. MONTGOMERY, *writer*

**# 125**

. . . [S]ail on solar wind. Hone and spread your spirit till you yourself are a sail, whetted, translucent, broadside to the merest puff.

—ANNIE DILLARD, *writer*

**#126**

# Set wide the window. Let me drink the day.

—**EDITH WHARTON,** *writer*

**# 127**

Each day I go to my studio full of joy; in the evening when obliged to stop because of darkness I can scarcely wait for the morning to come . . . if I cannot give myself to my dear painting I am miserable.

—WILLIAM-ALDOPHE BOUGUEREAU, *painter*

**# 128**
.........

Then let us laugh. It is the cheapest luxury man enjoys, and, as Charles Lamb says, "is worth a hundred groans in any state of the market."
It stirs up the blood, expands the chest, electrifies the nerves, clears away the cobwebs from the brain, and gives

the whole system a shock
to which the voltaic-
pile is as nothing. Nay,
its delicious alchemy
converts even tears into
the quintessence of
merriment, and makes
wrinkles themselves
expressive of youth
and frolic.

—WILLIAM MATTHEWS, *poet*

*#129*

We either
make ourselves
happy or
miserable.
The amount
of work is
the same.

—CARLOS CASTANEDA, *writer*

# 130
••••••••

Peace, happiness
and joy is possible
during the time
I drink my tea.

—THÍCH NHẤT HẠNH, *Buddhist monk*

**#131**

# Just tell yourself, Duckie, you're really quite lucky!

—**Dr. Seuss,** *writer/illustrator*

# #132

So you're made of detritus [from exploded stars]. Get over it. Or better yet, celebrate it. After all, what nobler thought can one cherish than that the universe lives within us all?

—NEIL deGRASSE TYSON, *physicist*

**# 133**

# Hey, I've got nothing to do today but smile.

—**PAUL SIMON**, *musician/songwriter*

# 134

# Just play. Have fun. Enjoy the game.

—MICHAEL JORDAN, *basketball player*

# *135*

Why do they not teach you that time is a finger snap and an eye blink, and that you should not allow a moment to pass you by without taking joyous, ecstatic note of it, not wasting a single moment of its swift, breakneck circuit?

—PAT CONROY, *writer*

**#136**

# The sun is always shining someplace.

—MUHAMMAD ALI, *boxer*

## #137

Today you're here and
nothing you can do
will change that. Today
you're alive and here and
honored, and blessed
with good fortune.
Look at this sunset,
it's beautiful, *neh?* This
sunset exists. Tomorrow
does not exist. There is
only *now*. Please look.

It is so beautiful and
it will never happen
ever again, never, not
*this* sunset, never in all
infinity. Lose yourself
in it, make yourself one
with nature and do not
worry about *karma,*
yours, mine, or that
of the village.

—JAMES CLAVELL, *writer*

**#138**
·········

Happiness is like swallows in Spring. It may come and nest under your eaves or it may not. You cannot command it. When you expect to be happy you are not, when you don't expect to be happy there's suddenly Easter in your soul, though it be midwinter.

—ELIZABETH GOUDGE, *writer*

**#139**

I am grateful to those who are keepers of the groove. The babies and the grandmas who hang on to it and help us remember when we forget that HERE— any kind of dancing is better than no dancing at all.

—LYNDA BARRY, *cartoonist*

## #140

You can choose to focus on the surprises and pleasures, or the frustrations. And you can choose to appreciate the smallest scraps of experience, the everyday moments, or to value only the grandest, most stirring ones. Ultimately, the real question is whether you want to be happy.

—CHRIS HADFIELD, *astronaut*

# #141

# It is no bad thing celebrating a simple life.

—J.R.R. TOLKIEN, *writer/professor*

# #142

The storm is over, there is sunlight in my heart. I have a glass of wine and sit thinking of what has passed.

—P. G. WODEHOUSE, *humorist*

**#143**

# Throw your dreams into space like a kite, and you do not know what it will bring back, a new life, a new friend, a new love, a new country.

—**ANAÏS NIN,** *writer*

**#144**

But this is what I'm finding, in glimpses and flashes: this is it. This is it, in the best possible way. That thing I'm waiting for, that adventure, that movie-score-worthy experience unfolding gracefully. This is it. Normal, daily life ticking by on our streets and sidewalks, in our houses and apartments, in our beds and at our dinner tables, in our dreams and prayers and fights and secrets—this pedestrian life is the most precious thing any of us will ever experience.

—SHAUNA NIEQUIST, *writer*

**#145**

# Dwell on the beauty of life. Watch the stars, and see yourself running with them.

—**MARCUS AURELIUS,** *emperor/philosopher*

# 146

Seize the moment.
Remember all
those women on
the *Titanic* who
waved off the
dessert cart.

—**ERMA BOMBECK,** *humorist*

# 147

People from a
planet without
flowers would
think we must
be mad with joy
the whole time to
have such things
about us.

—IRIS MURDOCH, *writer*

**#148**

*Life* is what
you celebrate.
All of it.
Even its end.

—JOANNE HARRIS, *writer*

**#149**

There are so many
people who don't know
what they want. And I
think that, in this world,
that's the only thing you
have to know—exactly
what you want. . . .
Doing what you were
born to do . . . That's
the way to be happy.

—AGNES MARTIN, *painter*

**#150**

# Be happy—if you're not even *happy* what's so good about surviving?

—TOM STOPPARD, *playwright*

**# 151**

I like to wake up
each morning
and not know
what I think,
that I may
reinvent myself
in some way.

—STEPHEN FRY, *comedian*

**#152**

I know that I am mortal by nature and ephemeral, but when I trace at my pleasure the windings to and fro of the heavenly bodies, I no longer touch earth with my feet. I stand in the presence of Zeus himself and take my fill of ambrosia.

—PTOLEMY, *astronomer*

# 153

Joy is what happens to us when we allow ourselves to recognize how good things really are.

—MARIANNE WILLIAMSON, *writer*

**# 154**

I'm far from being
a pessimist. . . .
On the contrary,
in spite of my
scars, I'm tickled
to death with life!

—EUGENE O'NEILL, *playwright*

# *155*

If the day and the night are such that you greet them with joy, and life emits a fragrance like flowers and sweet-scented herbs, is more elastic, more starry, more immortal—that is your success.

—HENRY DAVID THOREAU, *naturalist/writer*

**#156**

# Life is a beautiful, magnificent thing, even to a jellyfish.

—**CHARLIE CHAPLIN,** *actor/director*

*# 157*

# I still get wildly enthusiastic about little things . . . I play with leaves. I skip down the street and run against the wind.

—LEO BUSCAGLIA, *professor/writer*

**#158**

In a world where thrushes sing and willow trees are golden in the spring, boredom should have been included among the seven deadly sins.

—ELIZABETH GOUDGE, *writer*

**# 159**

# You need to let the little things that would ordinarily bore you suddenly thrill you.

—ANDY WARHOL, *artist*

# 160

Ah, life is a gate, a way, a path to Paradise anyway, why not live for fun and joy and love or some sort of girl by a fireside, why not go to your desire and LAUGH.

—JACK KEROUAC, *writer*

**# 161**

Before the tsunami,
I always looked to the
future. Always had
millions of lists of
things to do. If I were
talking to you, I would
not be here. I would be
thinking of something
that was coming up.
Now I'm talking to you.
I'm here. I'm present

with you. It's one of the most important things I learned: to be present, because in this moment I'm creating the future. If we don't live now, we are losing the opportunity to live. If we don't live now, we are missing life.

—PETRA NĚMCOVÁ, *model/humanitarian*

# *162*

I'm in London watching the wind blow through a tree, and it's a wonderful thing to see.

—HELEN MIRREN, *actress*

**#163**

I laugh every day.
There are days
when my laughs
are pretty hollow.
Dust comes out
of your mouth and
your bones make a
funny sound. But
I'm laughing.

—JAMES L. BROOKS, *filmmaker*

**#164**

Watch the sunrise at least once a year, put a lot of marshmallows in your hot chocolate, lie on your back and look at the stars, never buy a coffee table you can't put your feet on, never pass up a chance to jump on a trampoline, don't overlook life's small joys while searching for the big ones.

—H. JACKSON BROWN JR., *writer*

# #165

# There are flowers everywhere for those who want to see them.

—HENRI MATISSE, *artist*

**#166**

Try to learn to breathe deeply, really to taste food when you eat, and when you sleep, really to sleep. Try as much as possible to be wholly alive with all your might, and when you laugh, laugh like hell. And when you get angry, get good and angry. Try to be alive.

—WILLIAM SAROYAN, *writer*

**# 167**

A morning-glory
at my window
satisfies me
more than the
metaphysics of
books.

—WALT WHITMAN, *poet*

#168

And the corollary to carpe diem—a vein that runs deeply through the rock of poetry—is gratitude, gratitude for simply being alive, for having a day to seize. The taking of breath, the beating of the heart. Gratitude for the natural world around us—the massing clouds, the white ibis by the shore. In Barcelona a poetry competition is held every year. There are three prizes. The third prize is a rose made of silver, the second prize is a golden rose, and the first prize: a rose. A real rose. The flower itself. Think of that the next time the term "priorities" comes up.

—BILLY COLLINS, *poet*

### #169

I think it pisses God off if you walk by the color purple in a field somewhere and don't notice it. . . . People think pleasing God is all God cares about. But any fool living in the world can see it always trying to please us back.

—ALICE WALKER, *writer*

*# 170*

# Perhaps I am not I even if my little dog knows me but anyway I like what I have and now is today.

—GERTRUDE STEIN, *writer/critic*

*# 171*

If you see
the world
as beautiful,
thrilling and
mysterious, as
I think I do,
then you feel
quite alive.

—DAVID HOCKNEY, *artist*

# 172

Three o'clock
in the morning.
The soft April
night is looking at
my windows and
caressingly winking
at me with its stars.
I can't sleep, I am
so happy!

—ANTON CHEKHOV, *writer*

#173

Life is made up of moments, small pieces of glittering mica in a long stretch of gray cement. It would be wonderful if they came to us unsummoned, but particularly in lives as busy as the ones most of us lead now, that won't happen. We have to teach ourselves how to make room for them, to love them, and to live, really live.

—ANNA QUINDLEN, *writer*

# # 174

# Do anything, but let it produce joy.

—HENRY MILLER, *writer*

*# 175*

# Forever is composed of nows.

—EMILY DICKINSON, *poet*

# 176

... [T]here is a condition inside you which looks at the stars with amazement and awe. That listens to water with a river flowing, or water falling in rain and is lifted up by that and listens to a wonderful singer, wonderful musicians, listens to maybe Duke Ellington or Frank Sinatra or listens to Odetta and Mary J. Blige. Yes, and thinks whoo!

—MAYA ANGELOU, *writer*

*# 177*

Happiness
is sporadic.
It comes in
moments
and that's it.
Extract the
blood from
every moment.

—ROBERT REDFORD, *actor/director*

# 178

Enjoy your life.
No curse hangs
over you, nor did
it ever. No devil
chases after your
soul. Sing and
dance and be
merry.

—CHRISTOPHER PIKE, *writer*

**#179**

I wanted a perfect ending. . . .
Now I've learned the hard
way, that some poems don't
rhyme, and some stories
don't have a clear beginning,
middle, and end . . . [L]ife
is about not knowing,
having to change, taking the
moment and making the
best of it, without knowing
what's going to happen next.
Delicious ambiguity.

—GILDA RADNER, *comedian*

**#180**

Pay attention, don't let life go by you. Fall in love with the back of your cereal box.

—JERRY SEINFELD, *comedian*

### #181

Keep fighting for freedom and justice, beloveds, but don't you forget to have fun doin' it. Lord, let your laughter ring forth. Be outrageous, ridicule the 'fraidy-cats, rejoice in all the oddities that freedom can produce. And when you get through kickin' ass and celebratin' the sheer joy of a good fight, be sure to tell those who come after how much fun it was.

—**MOLLY IVINS**, *columnist*

# #182

# Too much of a good thing can be wonderful.

—MAE WEST, *actress*

**#183**

This is what makes me happy:
An evening in bed with a
good book. . . .
Any music-free restaurant. . . .
As you can see, it doesn't
take much to make me
happy. . . .
A good night's sleep. . . .
A grandson who offers
to clean the snow off
my driveway and also
fix my computer. . . .

—**ART BUCHWALD**, *columnist*

# 184

If only we'd stop trying to be happy we'd have a pretty good time.

—**EDITH WHARTON,** *writer*

*#185*

# The passing moment is all that we can be sure of; it is only common sense to extract its utmost value from it . . .

—W. SOMERSET MAUGHAM, *writer*

**#186**

# Nobody really cares if you're miserable, so you might as well be happy.

—CYNTHIA NELMS, *artist*

**#187**

Life was about spending time together, about having the time to walk together holding hands, talking quietly as they watched the sun go down. It wasn't glamorous, but it was, in many ways, the best that life had to offer.

—**NICHOLAS SPARKS**, *writer*

**#188**

I can't be smug,
because I know
that you can lose
anything at any
point. And I can't
be angry, because
I haven't lost it.

—MICHAEL J. FOX, *actor*

**#189**

There is ecstasy in paying attention. You can get into a kind of Wordsworthian openness to the world, where you see in everything the essence of holiness.

—ANNE LAMOTT, *writer*

# #190

We're so busy
watching out
for what's just
ahead of us that
we don't take
time to enjoy
where we are.

—BILL WATTERSON, *cartoonist*

The aim of life is to live, and to live means to be aware, joyously, drunkenly, serenely, divinely aware.

—HENRY MILLER, *writer*

*#192*

Lend your ears to music, open your eyes to painting, and . . . stop thinking!

—**WASSILY KANDINSKY**, *artist*

#### #193

In the same way that one has to accept the weather, so one has to accept how one feels about life sometimes. "Today's a crap day," is a perfectly realistic approach. It's all about finding a kind of mental umbrella. "Hey-ho, it's raining inside: it isn't my fault and there's nothing I can do about it, but sit it out. But the sun may well come out tomorrow and when it does, I shall take full advantage."

—STEPHEN FRY, *comedian*

# 194

Joy is to fun what the deep sea is to a puddle. It's a feeling inside that can hardly be contained.

—TERRY PRATCHETT, *writer*

**#195**

The longer I live, the more beautiful life becomes. If you foolishly ignore beauty, you will soon find yourself without it. Your life will be impoverished. But if you invest in beauty, it will remain with you all the days of your life.

—FRANK LLOYD WRIGHT, *architect*

**#196**

# Very occasionally, if you really pay attention, life doesn't suck.

—JOSS WHEDON, *director*

#197

You can become
blind by seeing each
day as a similar one.
Each day is a different
one, each day brings
a miracle of its own.
It's just a matter of
paying attention to
this miracle.

—PAULO COELHO, *writer*

**#198**

Many people need desperately to receive this message: "I feel and think much as you do, care about many of the things you care about, although most people do not care about them. You are not alone."

—KURT VONNEGUT, *writer*

**# 199**

# A happy man is too satisfied with the present to dwell too much on the future.

—ALBERT EINSTEIN, *physicist*

# *# 200*
........

Even if
happiness
forgets you a
little bit, never
completely
forget about it.

—JACQUES PRÉVERT, *poet*

**# 201**

# If you can't make it better, you can laugh at it.

—**ERMA BOMBECK,** *humorist*

# 202

You should eat delicious things while you can still eat them, go to wonderful places while you still can . . . and not have evenings where you say to yourself, "What am I doing here? Why am I here? I am bored witless!"

—NORA EPHRON, *writer/journalist*

*# 203*

When you dance,
your purpose is not
to get to a certain
place on the floor.
It's to enjoy each
step along the way.

—WAYNE DYER, *self-help writer/
motivational speaker*

# 204

# To draw, you must close your eyes and sing.

—**PABLO PICASSO**, *artist*

**#205**

Remember that there are only three kinds of things anyone need ever do. (1) Things we *ought* to do (2) Things we've *got* to do (3) Things we *like* doing. I say this because some people seem to spend so much of their time doing things for none of the three reasons, things like reading books they don't like because other people read them.

—C. S. LEWIS, *writer*

# #206

For like a shaft, clear and cold, the thought pierced him that in the end the Shadow was only a small and passing thing: there was light and high beauty for ever beyond its reach.

—J.R.R. TOLKIEN, *writer/professor*

*# 207*

We are all
worms,
but I do
believe
I am a
glow-worm.

—**WINSTON CHURCHILL,** *statesman*

**#208**

"Dear old world,"
she murmured,
"you are very lovely,
and I am glad to be
alive in you."

—L. M. MONTGOMERY, *writer*

**#209**

# Write it on your heart that every day is the best day in the year.

—**RALPH WALDO EMERSON,** *poet/essayist*

**# 210**

It is a visual joy to watch the grays in the morning light turn to color by the sun, watch evenings with color-saturated shadows; see how the noonday sun flattens, how colors sing on a rainy day.

—Jo Scott-B, *artist*

*# 211*

I know the joy
of fishes in the
river through
my own joy,
as I go walking
along the same
river.

—CHUANG TZU, *philosopher*

**# 212**

It is not in doing what you like, but in liking what you do that is the secret of happiness.

—J. M. BARRIE, *writer*

# 213

# You live once and life is wonderful, so eat the damned red velvet cupcake.

—EMMA STONE, *actress*

**# 214**

Have you ever seen the dawn?
Not a dawn groggy with lack
of sleep or hectic with mindless
obligations and you about to
rush off on an early adventure
or business, but full of deep
silence and absolute clarity of
perception? A dawning which
you truly observe, degree by
degree. It is the most amazing
moment of birth. And more
than anything it can spur you
to action. Have a burning day.

—VERA NAZARIAN, *writer*

# 215

One regret dear world, that I am determined not to have when I am lying on my deathbed is that I did not kiss you enough.

—**HAFIZ**, *poet*

**# 216**

# I believe in dancing.

—ROBERT FULGHUM, *writer*

*# 217*

There is always something
to celebrate, whether
it is the first green tip
of a snowdrop pushing
up or the gathering of
suncrisped shirts fresh off
the clothesline. There are
flowers to count and fruit
to harvest.

Be conscious and hold
on as we spin around the
sun one more time.

—NIKKI MCCLURE, *artist*

# 218

I finally
figured out
the only
reason to be
alive is to
enjoy it.

—RITA MAE BROWN, *writer*

# 219

# Fun
# is good.

—DR. SEUSS, *writer/illustrator*

# 220

It's like, wait a minute, this is it. This is your life. We only have moments. This moment's as good as any other. It's perfect.

—JON KABAT-ZINN, *professor/medical scientist*

# 221

Stuff your eyes with wonder . . . live as if you'd drop dead in ten seconds. See the world. It's more fantastic than any dream made or paid for in factories.

—RAY BRADBURY, *writer*

# 222

Sometimes people let
the same problem make
them miserable for years
when they could just say,
"So what." That's one of
my favorite things to say.
"So what."

—ANDY WARHOL, *artist*

# #223

# Exuberance is beauty.

—**WILLIAM BLAKE**, *writer*

**# 224**

My advice to
you is not to
inquire why or
whither, but just
enjoy your ice
cream while it's
on your plate.

—THORNTON WILDER, *writer*

## # 225

The reality is that we're all in the wilderness and we have to survive on our own, and things constantly change, and if we don't accept that, then we're just trying to fool ourselves. But the beauty of wilderness is that sometimes you can wake up in the morning and feel so sweet and whole.

—SOPHIE B. HAWKINS, *singer/songwriter*

**# 226**

If you have good
thoughts they will
shine out of your
face like sunbeams
and you will always
look lovely.

—ROALD DAHL, *writer*

# 227

I say, "Every day is like a Saturday morning"—you got a great feeling, and it grows and grows and grows.

—DAVID LYNCH, *filmmaker*

**#228**

The moment one gives close attention to anything, even a blade of grass, it becomes a mysterious, awesome, indescribably magnificent world in itself.

—HENRY MILLER, *writer*

**# 229**

I had a very late eureka experience not so long ago. I was up around where I live and I looked out at the blue skies and the clouds and I realized that this was paradise. And that's something pretty big to hang on to.

—JACK NICHOLSON, *actor*

**# 230**

# The universe is not outside of you. Look inside yourself; everything that you want you already are.

—RUMI, *Sufi mystic*

*# 231*

"It's snowing still,"
said Eeyore gloomily.
"So it is."
"And freezing."
"Is it?"
"Yes," said Eeyore.
"However," he said,
brightening up a little,
"we haven't had an
earthquake lately."

—A. A. MILNE, *writer*

# 232

We should live every day like people who have just been rescued from the moon.

—THÍCH NHẤT HẠNH, *Buddhist monk*

# 233

I think the thing to do is enjoy the ride while you're on it.

—**JOHNNY DEPP,** *actor*

**# 234**

# The moments of happiness we enjoy take us by surprise. It is not that we seize them, but that they seize us.

—ASHLEY MONTAGU, *anthropologist*

# 235

We must risk delight. We can do without pleasure, but not delight. Not enjoyment.

—JACK GILBERT, *poet*

# 236

Seize from
every moment
its unique
novelty, and
do not prepare
your joys.

—ANDRÉ GIDE, *writer*

*# 237*

Be fully awake to
everything about
you & the more
you can appreciate,
& get a full measure
of joy & happiness
out of life.

—JACKSON POLLOCK, *artist*

# # 238

Every place
is under the
stars, every
place is the
center of
the world.

—JOHN BURROUGHS, *naturalist*

**# 239**

With all its sham, drudgery, and broken dreams, it is still a beautiful world. Be cheerful. Strive to be happy.

—MAX EHRMANN, *poet/attorney*

# 240

There's a sunrise and a sunset every single day, and they're absolutely free. Don't miss so many of them.

—JO WALTON, *writer*

# Dance, creature! Put down your pen, lift up your limbs, and dance to greet another golden morning.

—**WOODY HARRELSON,** *actor*

# 242

Cheerfulness is
an achievement,
and hope is
something to
celebrate.

—ALAIN DE BOTTON, *writer*

# Feet, what do I need you for when I have wings to fly?

—FRIDA KAHLO, *artist*

**#244**

Get a life in which you are generous. Look around at the azaleas making fuchsia star bursts in spring; look at a full moon hanging silver in a black sky on a cold night. And realize that life is glorious, and that you have no business taking it for granted.

—ANNA QUINDLEN, *writer*

**#245**

# For God's sake, keep your eyes open.

—**WILLIAM S. BURROUGHS,** *writer*

*# 246*

*There's always a reason to smile.* Find it. After all, you're really lucky just to be alive. Life is short. More and more, I agree with my little brother. He always reminds me: "We're not here for a long time; we're here for a good time."

—BOB PARSONS, *business executive*

*# 247*
.........

# This snowy morning
# That black crow
# I hate so much. . .
# But he's so beautiful!

—MATSUO BASHŌ, *poet*

**#248**

Let us be grateful to the people who make us happy; they are the charming gardeners who make our souls blossom.

—MARCEL PROUST, *writer*

**#249**

# Lean back and be loved by all that is already loving you.

—**LEONARD COHEN**, *singer/songwriter*

# 250

# The best way to pay for a lovely moment is to enjoy it.

—RICHARD BACH, *writer*

*# 251*

# Remember that your natural state is joy.

—**WAYNE DYER,** *self-help writer/ motivational speaker*

# 252

To look at everything always as though you were seeing it either for the first or last time: Thus is your time on earth filled with glory.

—BETTY SMITH, *writer*

**#253**

We were made to
enjoy music, to enjoy
beautiful sunsets, to
enjoy looking at the
billows of the sea and
to be thrilled with a
rose that is bedecked
with dew.

—**DESMOND TUTU**, *religious leader*

**# 254**

Be happy
whenever you
can manage it.
Enjoy yourself.
It's lighter than
you think.

—CORITA KENT, *artist/activist*

**# 255**

Laughter is wine for the soul—laughter soft, or loud and deep, tinged through with seriousness . . . the hilarious declaration made by man that life is worth living.

—SEÁN O'CASEY, *playwright*

**# 256**

# Practice kindness all day to everybody and you will realize you're already in heaven now.

—JACK KEROUAC, *writer*

# 257

We pray for the big things and forget to give thanks for the ordinary, small (and yet really not small) gifts.

—DIETRICH BONHOEFFER,
*religious leader*

# 258

The sun shines not on us but in us. The rivers flow not past, but through us, thrilling, tingling, vibrating every fiber and cell of the substance of our bodies, making them glide and sing. The trees wave and the flowers bloom in our bodies as well as our souls, and every bird song, wind song, and tremendous storm song of the rocks in the heart of the mountains is our song, our very own, and sings our love.

—JOHN MUIR, *naturalist*

# 259

I like it when a flower or a little tuft of grass grows through a crack in the concrete. It's so f\*\*\*in' heroic.

—GEORGE CARLIN, *comedian*

**#260**

# I don't think of all the misery, but of the beauty that still remains.

—**ANNE FRANK**, *diarist*

**# 261**

You dance love, and you dance joy, and you dance dreams. And I know if I can make you smile by jumping over a couple of couches or running through a rainstorm, then I'll be very glad to be a song and dance man.

—GENE KELLY, *dancer/actor*

# #262

When I was 5 years old, my mother always told me that happiness was the key to life. When I went to school, they asked me what I wanted to be when I grew up. I wrote down "happy." They told me I didn't understand the assignment, and I told them they didn't understand life.

—JOHN LENNON,
*musician/songwriter*

*# 263*

# The earth has music for those who listen.

—WILLIAM SHAKESPEARE, *playwright*

**# 264**

# Don't just live. Be that other thing connected to death. Be life. Live all of your life. Understand it, see it, appreciate it. And have fun.

—JOSS WHEDON, *director*

**#265**

# Dreams come true. Without that possibility, nature would not incite us to have them.

—JOHN UPDIKE, *writer*

# 266

There are some days when I think I'm going to die from an overdose of satisfaction.

—**SALVADOR DALÍ,** *artist*

277

*#267*

You have to make your own happiness, wherever you are. Your job isn't going to make you happy, your spouse isn't going to make you happy, the weather isn't going to make you happy. . . . You have to decide what you want, and you have to find that way of doing it, whether or not the outside circumstances are going to participate in your success. . . . You have to be able to create your own happiness, period. And if you can't, then you need to find a good shrink who can help you figure out what it's going to take.

—DEBBIE MILLMAN, *designer*

**# 268**

I think happiness is what makes you pretty. Period. Happy people are beautiful. They become like a mirror and they reflect that happiness.

—**DREW BARRYMORE,** *actress*

# 269

Let us toast to animal pleasures, to escapism, to rain on the roof and instant coffee, to unemployment insurance and library cards, to absinthe and good-hearted landlords, to music and warm bodies and contraceptives . . . and to the "good life" whatever it is and wherever it happens to be.

—HUNTER S. THOMPSON, *journalist*

*# 270*

When we have learned
how to listen to trees,
then the brevity and
the quickness and the
childlike hastiness of
our thoughts achieve an
incomparable joy.

—HERMANN HESSE, *writer*

# 271

I've always thought that a big laugh is a really loud noise from the soul saying, "Ain't that the truth."

—QUINCY JONES, *record producer*

# 272

A clear horizon—nothing
to worry about on your
plate, only things that are
creative and not destructive.
. . . I can't bear quarreling,
I can't bear feelings between
people—I think hatred is
wasted energy, and it's all
non-productive. I'm very
sensitive—a sharp word,
said by a person, say, who
has a temper, if they're
close to me, hurts me for

days. I know we're only human, we do go in for these various emotions, call them negative emotions, but when all these are removed and you can look forward and the road is clear ahead, and now you're going to create something— I think that's as happy as I'll ever want to be.

—**ALFRED HITCHCOCK,** *filmmaker*

**# 273**

# There is a sort of elation about sunlight on the upper part of a house.

—EDWARD HOPPER, *artist*

**# 274**

# Now and then it's good to pause in our pursuit of happiness and just be happy.

—GUILLAUME APOLLINAIRE, *poet*

# 275

In life, in true life, there can be nothing better than what is.

—LEO TOLSTOY, *writer*

**# 276**

In the external scheme of things, shining moments are as brief as the twinkling of an eye, yet such twinklings are what eternity is made of—moments when we human beings can say "I love you," "I'm proud of you," "I forgive you," "I'm grateful for you." That's what eternity is made of: invisible imperishable *good stuff.*

—**FRED ROGERS,** *children's TV host*

*# 277*

# When was the last time you looked at the stars with the wonder they deserve?

—Kris Kristofferson, *singer/songwriter*

**# 278**

You say grace before meals.
All right. But I say grace
before the concert and the
opera, and grace before the
play and pantomime, and
grace before I open a book,
and grace before sketching,
painting, swimming, fencing,
boxing, walking, playing,
dancing and grace before
I dip the pen in the ink.

—G. K. CHESTERTON, *writer*

# Delight in the little things.

—RUDYARD KIPLING, *writer*

# 280

You have so much to enjoy and to be, and to do.

—J.R.R. TOLKIEN, *writer/professor*

*# 281*

# The living moment is everything.

—D. H. LAWRENCE, *writer*

# #282

Listen to the birds. That's where all the music comes from. Birds know everything about how it should sound and where that sound should come from. And watch hummingbirds. They fly really fast, but a lot of times they aren't going anywhere.

—**CAPTAIN BEEFHEART,** *musician*

**#283**

# Be happy for this moment. This moment is your life.

—OMAR KHAYYAM, *poet*

**#284**

# Your body is not a temple, it's an amusement park. Enjoy the ride.

—**ANTHONY BOURDAIN**, *chef/writer*

# *285*

At some point in life the world's beauty becomes enough. You don't need to photograph, paint, or even remember it. It is enough.

—TONI MORRISON, *writer*

# #286

Though it may feel otherwise, enjoying life is no more dangerous than apprehending it with continuous anxiety and gloom.

—ALAIN DE BOTTON, *writer*

*# 287*

# Happiness is right in front of you.

—**Hafiz,** *poet*

**#288**

# The most wasted of all days is one without laughter.

—E. E. CUMMINGS, *poet*

*#289*

One of the things [Uncle Alex] found objectionable about human beings was that they so rarely noticed it when they were happy. He himself did his best to acknowledge it when times were sweet. We could be drinking lemonade in the shade of an apple tree in the summertime, and Uncle

Alex would interrupt the conversation to say, "If this isn't nice, what is?"

So I hope that you will do the same for the rest of your lives. When things are going sweetly and peacefully, please pause a moment, and then say out loud, "If this isn't nice, what is?"

—KURT VONNEGUT, *writer*

*# 290*

Give me a moment, because I like to cry for joy. It's so delicious...to cry for joy.

—CHARLES DICKENS, *writer*

Never before have I lived through a storm like the one this night. . . . The sea has a look of indescribable grandeur, especially when the sun falls on it. One feels as if one is dissolved and merged into Nature. Even more than usual, one feels the insignificance of the individual, and it makes one happy.

—ALBERT EINSTEIN, *physicist*

# #292

# Nobody cares if you can't dance well. Just get up and dance.

—MARTHA GRAHAM, *choreographer*

**#293**

# Don't put off till tomorrow what can be enjoyed today.

—JOSH BILLINGS, *humorist*

# 294

I have no
money, no
resources, no
hopes. I am
the happiest
man alive.

—HENRY MILLER, *writer*

*# 295*

The true way to live is
to enjoy every moment
as it passes and surely it
is in the everyday things
around us that the beauty
of life lies.

—Laura Ingalls Wilder, *writer*

**#296**

I believe in having fun first, and along the way, if you teach people, if you influence people, well and good.

—RAY BRADBURY, *writer*

# #297

# A man is happy so long as he chooses to be happy.

—ALEKSANDR SOLZHENITSYN, *writer*

*# 298*

# The time to be happy is now. The place to be happy is here.

—ROBERT GREEN INGERSOLL, *lawyer*

# 299

Happiness is excitement that has found a settling down place, but there is always a little corner that keeps flapping around.

—E. L. KONIGSBURG, *writer*

*#300*
••••••••

# Scatter joy!

—RALPH WALDO EMERSON, *poet/essayist*

**# 301**

How to be happy when you are miserable. Plant Japanese poppies with cornflowers and mignonette, and bed out the petunias among the sweet-peas so that they shall scent each other. See the sweet-peas coming up. Drink very good tea out of a thin Worcester cup of a colour between apricot and pink.

—**RUMER GODDEN,** *writer*

**# 302**

# The most important thing is to enjoy your life—be happy— it's all that matters.

—**AUDREY HEPBURN,** *actress/humanitarian*

# 303

I wouldn't waste a day, not an hour, not a moment. Take what you want . . . and damn caution. Live, enjoy. Feed ravenously. Or the biggest regret you'll have at the end of your life is wasted time.

—NORA ROBERTS, *writer*

**#304**

# Dance, even if you have nowhere to do it but your living room.

—MARY SCHMICH, *journalist*

# 305

I believe that life is a game, that life is a cruel joke, and that life is what happens when you're alive and that you might as well lie back and enjoy it.

—NEIL GAIMAN, *writer*

A passionate interest in
what you do is the secret
of enjoying life, perhaps
the secret of long life,
whether it is helping
old people or children,
or making cheese or
growing earthworms.

—JULIA CHILD, *chef*

*#307*

# If you're not having fun, you're doing something wrong.

—Groucho Marx, *comedian/producer*

*#308*
..........

By definition, you have
to live until you die.
Better to make that
life as complete and
enjoyable an experience
as possible, in case death
is shite, which I suspect
it will be.

—IRVINE WELSH, *writer*

**# 309**

Everything
in excess!
To enjoy the
flavor of life,
take big bites.
Moderation
is for monks.

—ROBERT A. HEINLEIN, *writer*

# #310

You have everything needed for the extravagant journey that is your life.

—CARLOS CASTANEDA, *anthropologist*

# 311

There are two things to aim at in life: first, to get what you want; and, after that, to enjoy it. Only the wisest of mankind achieve the second.

—LOGAN PEARSALL SMITH, *writer*

*# 312*

I believe that half the trouble in the world comes from people asking "What have I achieved?" rather than "What have I enjoyed?"

—WALTER FARLEY, *writer*

**# 313**

I began to realize how important it was to be an enthusiast in life. He taught me that if you are interested in something, no matter what it is, go at it full speed ahead. Embrace it with both arms, hug it, love it and above all become passionate about it. Lukewarm is no good. Hot is no good either. White hot and passionate is the only thing to be.

—**ROALD DAHL**, *writer*

# 314

If you spend your whole life waiting for the storm, you'll never enjoy the sunshine.

—MORRIS L. WEST, *anthropologist*

**# 315**

[It]'s all right to be happy . . . you don't have to be constantly manufacturing problems that you don't really have.

—JACK NICHOLSON, *actor*

# 316

# When I started counting my blessings, my whole life turned around.

—**WILLIE NELSON,** *singer/songwriter*

**# 317**

Life's a roller coaster.
Best damn ride in the
park. You don't close
your eyes, hold on and
wait for it to be over,
babe. You keep your
eyes open, lift your
hands straight up in
the air and enjoy the
ride for as long as
it lasts.

—**KRISTEN ASHLEY**, *writer*

# # 318

Man is fond of counting his troubles, but he does not count his joys. If he counted them up as he ought to, he would see that every lot has enough happiness provided for it.

—FYODOR DOSTOEVSKY, *writer*

# 319

When you take a flower in your hand and really look at it, it's your world for the moment.

—GEORGIA O'KEEFFE, *artist*

And to me also, who appreciate life, the butterflies, and soap-bubbles, and whatever is like them amongst us, seem most to enjoy happiness.

—**FRIEDRICH NIETZSCHE**, *philosopher*

# # 321

I think it's really tragic when
people get serious about stuff.
It's such an absurdity to take
anything really seriously. . . .
I make an honest attempt not
to take anything seriously:
I worked that attitude out
about the time I was eighteen,
I mean, what does it all mean
when you get right down to
it, what's the story here?
Being alive is so weird.

—**FRANK ZAPPA,** *musician/songwriter*

**# 322**

Observe the wonders as they occur around you. Don't claim them. Feel the artistry moving through, and be silent.

—RUMI, *Sufi mystic*

# 323

Clouds come floating into my life, no longer to carry rain or usher storm, but to add color to my sunset sky.

—RABINDRANATH TAGORE, *writer*

# 324

The earth was warm under me, and warm as I crumbled it through my fingers. Queer little red bugs came out and moved in slow squadrons around me. Their backs were polished vermilion, with black spots. I kept as still as I could. Nothing happened. I did not expect anything to happen. I was something that lay under the sun and felt it, like the pumpkins, and

I did not want to be anything
more. I was entirely happy.
Perhaps we feel like that
when we die and become
a part of something entire,
whether it is sun and air, or
goodness and knowledge. At
any rate, that is happiness; to
be dissolved into something
complete and great. When
it comes to one, it comes as
naturally as sleep.

—**WILLA CATHER,** *writer*

# 325

# So far, so good.

—KEITH RICHARDS, *rock musician*

You were given life;
it is your duty (and
also your entitlement
as a human being)
to find something
beautiful within life,
no matter how slight.

—ELIZABETH GILBERT, *writer*

# 327
•••••••

# Every day is great— it's a day extra.

—JAKE LaMOTTA, *boxer*

**# 328**

I don't look
ahead. I'm right
here with you. It's
a good way to be.

—**DANNY DeVITO,** *actor*

# 329

Something important is always about to happen. . . . And if not, you'd do well to act as if it were. You'll enjoy life better that way.

—JULIA QUINN, *writer*

# 330

# Today was good. Today was fun. Tomorrow is another one.

—DR. SEUSS, *writer/illustrator*

*# 331*
........

# Live, travel, adventure, bless, and don't be sorry.

—JACK KEROUAC, *writer*

**#332**

# All I can say about life is, Oh God, enjoy it!

—BOB NEWHART, *comedian*

# #333

Life is meant to be
fun, and joyous, and
fulfilling. May each of
yours be that—having
each of you as a child
of mine has certainly
been one of the good
things in my life. Know
that I've always loved
each of you with an
eternal, bottomless

love. A love that has nothing to do with each other, for I feel my love for each of you is total and all-encompassing. Please watch out for each other and love and forgive everybody. It's a good life, enjoy it.

—JIM HENSON, *puppeteer (in a letter to his children to be read after his death)*

**#334**

# I can hardly wait for tomorrow, it means a new life for me each and every day.

—**STANLEY KUNITZ,** *poet*

# 335

You know Dalton Trumbo? He wrote *Johnny Got His Gun.* He was one of the blacklisted writers. Spent time in prison. Lost everything. Got everything back. Wonderful fellow. The last thing he said to me was "Don't forget to be happy."

—**DONALD SUTHERLAND,** *actor*

# 336

The sun is still there . . . even if clouds drift over it. Once you have experienced the reality of sunshine you may weep, but you will never feel ice about your heart again.

—ELIZABETH GOUDGE, *writer*

# 337

All that I ever hope to say, is that I love the world.

—E. B. WHITE, *writer*

# WHO'S QUOTED

**Muhammad Ali (1942– ):** American boxer. Ali is a three-time world heavyweight boxing champion. He is also renowned for his quick-witted repartee.

**Laurie Halse Anderson (1961– ):** American writer. Anderson is best known for her children's and young adult novels that deal with difficult topics, such as rape and academic pressures.

**Maya Angelou (1928–2014):** American writer, poet, and actress. Angelou is the acclaimed author of the multivolume memoir detailing an African American childhood, including the bestseller *I Know Why the Caged Bird Sings.*

**Guillaume Apollinaire (1880–1918):** Polish-born French writer. Apollinaire is considered one of the most important poets of the twentieth century. He was a major leader of the literary avant-garde. He influenced Futurist, Cubist, Dadaist, and particularly Surrealist movements.

**Kristen Ashley (1968– ):** American writer. Ashley is best known for her romantic fiction.

**W. H. Auden (1907–1973):** Anglo American poet and essayist. Auden is considered one of the greatest writers of the twentieth century. He won the Pulitzer Prize for *The Age of Anxiety.*

**Marcus Aurelius Antoninus Augustus (121–180 C.E.):** Roman emperor and philosopher. Aurelius is known as one of Rome's greatest Caesars. He is the author of the Stoic philosophy classic *The Meditations,* which focuses on duty and a calm acceptance of fate.

**Richard Bach** (1936– ): American writer. Bach wrote the huge 1970s bestseller *Jonathan Livingston Seagull*, which espouses that human potential is unlimited. An avid pilot, he often combines flying with spirituality in his novels.

**J. M. Barrie (Sir James Matthew Barrie, 1st Baronet OM)** (1860–1937): Scottish novelist and playwright. Barrie is the creator of the childhood classic *Peter Pan*.

**Lynda Barry** (1956– ): American cartoonist and writer. Barry is best known for her illustrated novels, including *One! Hundred! Demons!* and *What It Is*, which encourages readers to discover their own creativity. She is also known for her weekly comic *Ernie Pook's Comeek*.

**Drew Barrymore** (1975– ): American actress. She is a member of the famed Barrymore family of actors. Barrymore got her start as a child actress, notably in *E.T.: The Extra-Terrestrial*. After her descent into substance abuse, she reemerged as a performer in a number of hits. Barrymore established her own successful production company.

**Matsuo Bashō** (1644–1694): Japanese poet. Bashō was a master of the haiku form of poetry, but he himself preferred his renku forms of collaborative linked verse. The impressionistic and concise nature of his works have greatly influenced modern poets.

**Gregory Benford** (1941– ): American astrophysicist and writer of science fiction. Benford is best known for his Galactic Center Saga, a series of novels set in a galaxy where organic life is at war with electromechanical life.

**Elizabeth Berg** (1948– ): American writer. Originally a nurse, Berg won a competition in *Parents* magazine. She became a bestselling and award-winning novelist—best known for her trilogy about twelve-year-old Katie Nash.

**Milton Berle (1908–2002):** American comedian and actor. Born in New York City, he began performing at age five; several years later was a regular on the vaudeville circuit (accompanied by his mother); later achieved national fame on television where he was known to millions as Uncle Miltie.

**Wendell Berry (1934– ):** American writer and environmental activist. Berry bases his life and writing on his own relationship to the land. His novels and nonfiction works center on environmental, pacifist, and sustainable themes.

**Josh Billings (pseudonym of Henry Wheeler Shaw) (1818–1885):** American humorist. In his era, Billings was second only to Mark Twain in fame. He wrote folksy essays in the slang of the times.

**William Blake (1757–1827):** English writer and artist. Blake was largely unrecognized in his own day. He is now regarded as a seminal figure in the Romantic movement—a visionary, mystical thinker, with immense influence on later generations.

**Art Blakey (1919–1990):** American jazz drummer and bandleader. Blakey was one of the inventors of modern bebop drumming. His band, Art Blakey and the Jazz Messengers, was a training ground for generations of jazz musicians. He was inducted into the Jazz Hall of Fame and the Grammy Hall of Fame.

**Amy Bloom (1953– ):** American writer. Bloom is best known for her short stories, novels (especially her breakout novel, *Away*), and children's fiction. She has also worked as a psychotherapist and as a professor of creative writing.

**Erma Bombeck (1927–1996):** American humorist. Bombeck gained fame as a newspaper columnist writing about daily life in the suburban U.S. She also wrote several bestsellers, chiefly collections of her essays. She was a prominent backer of the Equal Rights Amendment.

**Dietrich Bonhoeffer (1906–1945):** German pastor and theologian. Bonhoeffer was a prominent writer on the role of Christianity in secular society, and a staunch opponent of Nazism. He was arrested and hanged by the Nazis shortly before the end of World War II.

**Alain de Botton (1969– ):** Swiss/British philosopher, writer, and television presenter. De Botton is best known for showing how philosophy can be relevant to everyday life.

**William-Adolphe Bouguereau (1825–1905):** French artist and academic painter. A traditionalist realist painter, often of mythological scenes, Bouguereau enjoyed great popularity but was reviled by the Impressionists. He fell out of favor in the 1900s, but recently his works are undergoing a revival.

**Anthony Bourdain (1956– ):** American chef, writer, and TV host. Bourdain is best known for his book *Kitchen Confidential,* his TV show highlighting world cuisines, and his advocacy of local and peasant foods.

**Ray Bradbury (1920–2012):** American science fiction writer. Bradbury is best known for his dystopian classic of book-burning, *Fahrenheit 451,* as well as numerous other novels and short stories, many of which have been made into films, including *The Martian Chronicles.*

**James L. Brooks (1940– ):** American filmmaker. Brooks made his name creating *The Mary Tyler Moore Show,* one of the first TV shows about a single working woman. He won three Academy Awards for the film *Terms of Endearment.*

**H. Jackson Brown Jr. (1940– ):** American writer. Brown is best known for his huge bestseller, *Life's Little Instruction Book.* Before becoming a full-time writer, he was the creative director of a Nashville advertising agency.

**Rita Mae Brown (1944– ):** American writer. Her first novel, *Rubyfruit Jungle,* was pioneering in its depiction of explicit lesbian themes.

**Art Buchwald (1925–2007):** American humorist. Buchwald was a Pulitzer Prize–winning columnist for *The Washington Post,* and was syndicated internationally.

**Jimmy Buffett (1946– ):** American singer and songwriter. Buffett is known for his humorous island escapist music, exemplified by his hit song "Margaritaville." He also owns restaurants based on the same theme.

**Charles Bukowski (1920–1994):** German-born American writer. Bukowski was acclaimed by *The New York Times,* among many others, as the "laureate of American lowlife." He was known for his gritty poems, short stories, and novels on ordinary lives of Americans, especially in his home city of Los Angeles, and on their drinking, work, and relationships.

**Frances Hodgson Burnett (1849–1924):** English writer. Burnett is best known for her sentimental children's fiction, *Little Lord Fauntleroy, A Little Princess,* and *The Secret Garden.*

**John Burroughs (1837–1921):** American writer and naturalist. Burroughs wrote popular essays on natural history, often about his beloved Catskill (New York) wilderness, as well as on philosophy, religion, and other topics. He was active in the conservation movement.

**William S. Burroughs (1914–1997):** American writer. Burroughs is known for his innovative technique, including the "cut-up," in which words and phrases are cut out and pasted together to form pages. He was the leading influence on the Beat Generation writers. His most famous works are the autobiographical *Junkie* and the surrealistic *Naked Lunch.*

**Leo Buscaglia (1924–1998):** American professor, writer, and motivational speaker. Buscaglia focused on the power of love. His books on this topic were bestsellers.

**Candace Bushnell (1958– ):** American columnist, writer, and producer. Bushnell wrote the "Sex and the City" column for *The New York Observer*, which was adapted into the bestselling *Sex and the City* essay collection and the hit TV series and films of the same name.

**John Calvin (1509–1564):** French theologian and pastor. Calvin was one of the key figures of the Protestant Reformation. He was the founder of the Protestant Calvinist branch, now represented by the Reformed, Congregational, and Presbyterian churches.

**Albert Camus (1913–1960):** Algerian-born French writer. Camus was the winner of a Nobel Prize. He was considered a prominent existentialist writer, though he himself rejected the term. Camus was fascinated by the seeming senselessness of life. He wrote that he was devoted to opposing the philosophy of nihilism.

**Captain Beefheart (stage name of Don Van Vliet) (1941–2010):** American musician, singer, and songwriter. Captain Beefheart is known as one of rock's most innovative musicians. He recorded thirteen acclaimed albums of what *Rolling Stone* termed "a sort of modern chamber music for rock bands."

**George Carlin (1937–2008):** American comedian. Carlin was known as the dean of counterculture comedians. He transformed his successful stand-up comedy into highly popular, satirical, cynical, and insightful looks at modern society. His famous "Seven Words You Can Never Say on Television" comedy routine was part of a radio censorship case that made its way to the U.S. Supreme Court.

**Dale Carnegie (1888–1955):** American self-help writer and lecturer. Carnegie was born into poverty on a Missouri farm. He rose to fame and wealth through his teachings on "How to Win Friends and Influence People," also the title of one of his bestselling books, still highly popular today.

**Carlos Castaneda (1925–1998):** Peruvian American anthropologist. He is best known for his authorship of a series of books on shamanism, focusing on his training with a Yaqui "Man of Knowledge."

**Willa Cather (1873–1947):** Pulitzer prize–winning American novelist. Cather wrote vivid depictions of pioneer life on the Great Plains based on her own experiences homesteading with her family in Nebraska.

**Charlie Chaplin (1889–1977):** English actor and director. A stage performer as a child, Chaplin went on to Hollywood, where he became the king of silent comedy with his portrayal of the well-loved Little Tramp character. With the advent of sound, he continued filmmaking and experimenting with the new medium. Chaplin left the U.S. in the 1950s because of problems caused by his left-wing politics and subsequently settled in Switzerland. He was knighted in 1975.

**Anton Chekhov (1860–1904):** Russian author and physician. Chekhov is considered one of the best and most innovative short-story writers (an early user of stream of consciousness). His work includes the play *The Cherry Orchard.* He practiced as a doctor throughout most of his life and famously said: "Medicine is my lawful wife and literature my mistress."

**G. K. (Gilbert Keith) Chesterton (1874–1936):** English writer of novels, poems, short stories, and nonfiction. Chesterton is noted for his wit and sense of humor, his Christian Catholic apologetics, and his Father Brown detective stories.

**Julia Child (1912–2004):** American chef, food writer, and television host. Child served in the OSS during World War II. She began her culinary career at the Cordon Bleu and later opened a cooking school. Child popularized French cooking on her hit TV show and through numerous cookbooks.

**Chuang Tzu (c. 369–286 B.C.E.):** Chinese Taoist philosopher. Chuang Tzu lived a hermit's life, yet was widely known for his ideas. He reportedly was offered a prime ministership, but turned it down, saying: "I prefer the enjoyment of my own free will."

**Winston Churchill (1874–1965):** British politician and writer. Churchill was prime minister of Great Britain from 1940–1945 and 1951–1955. He was instrumental in resisting Nazi advances in World War II, and was the winner of the Nobel Prize in Literature in 1953 for his voluminous histories.

**Cassandra Clare (pseudonym of Judith Rumelt) (1973– ):** American writer. Clare is best known for her young adult urban fantasy series The Mortal Instruments.

**James Clavell (1924–1994):** Australian-born British/American author and filmmaker. Clavell is best known for his bestselling Asian epic novels, including *Tai-Pan* and *Shōgun*, and such films as *To Sir, With Love.*

**John Cleese (1939– ):** English actor and humorist. Cleese cofounded the hit comedy group Monty Python, and starred in and cowrote the classic comedy series *Fawlty Towers* as well as the hit film *A Fish Called Wanda*. He co-owns a production company.

**Paulo Coelho (1947– ):** Brazilian novelist and lyricist. Coelho rebelled against his parents' wishes for a traditional lifestyle. He was sent to an insane asylum from which he escaped. He later quit law school and traveled South America as a hippie. His life was transformed during a pilgrimage to Santiago de Compostela. Shortly after, Coelho wrote his famous book *The Alchemist*. Altogether his acclaimed novels have sold over 150 million copies.

**Leonard Cohen** (1934– ): Canadian singer, songwriter, and poet. Cohen is noted for his complex explorations of human loneliness and religious yearnings.

**Colette** (1873–1954): French novelist and memoirist. Colette is famous for her bohemian lifestyle. She performed in acting troupes, as a mime, and as a music hall dancer. She gained notoriety for her lesbian affair. Her most famous works include the Claudine series, *Chéri*, and *Gigi*.

**Billy Collins** (1941– ): American poet, English professor, and Poet Laureate of the United States from 2001–2003. Collins is known as the "most popular poet in America." His poems are often conversational and witty, but with profound undertones.

**Pat Conroy** (1945– ): American writer. Conroy is a self-described Southern "military brat" whose background informs his writing. He is the author of several acclaimed bestsellers.

**E. E. Cummings** (1894–1962): American writer and painter. Cummings is considered among the most innovative (and popular) twentieth-century poets. He experimented with form, punctuation, spelling, and syntax to create a highly individual style, often with humor.

**Roald Dahl** (1916–1990): British writer. Dahl's short stories and especially his bestselling children's novels, including *James and the Giant Peach*, *Charlie and the Chocolate Factory*, and *Matilda*, are known for their dark, humorous twists.

**Salvador Dalí (Salvador Felipe Jacinto Dalí y Domenech, 1st Marqués de Dalí de Pubol)** (1904–1989): Spanish surrealist painter, graphic artist, and designer. Dalí cultivated eccentricity and exhibitionism in his life and art. He described his paintings as "hand-painted dream photographs."

**Rubén Darío** (1867–1916): Nicaraguan poet, journalist, and diplomat.

Darío was called the "Prince of Castilian Letters." He initiated the modernist twentieth-century Spanish American literary movement called Modernismo that revolutionized Spanish literature on both sides of the Atlantic by experimenting with rhythm, meter, and imagery.

**Miles Davis (1926–1991):** American jazz trumpeter, composer, arranger, and bandleader. Davis is one of the most influential musicians of the twentieth century. Ever innovative, he was most famous for the "Birth of Cool" sessions that revolutionized jazz.

**Richard Dawkins (1941– ):** English biologist and writer. Dawkins is best known for his gene-centered view of evolution, his attacks on the belief in God, and his defense of atheism.

**Johnny Depp (1963– ):** American actor and film producer. Depp rose to fame as a teen idol in television's *21 Jump Street.* He turned to more challenging roles in film, including *Edward Scissorhands* as well as the popular Pirates of the Caribbean movies.

**Danny DeVito (1944– ):** American actor and filmmaker. DeVito's first big break came when he played dispatcher Louis De Palma in the hit television series *Taxi.* He went on to play numerous award-winning character roles in hit films such as *Romancing the Stone* and *Throw Momma from the Train.* DeVito is the cofounder of the major production company Jersey Films.

**Charles Dickens (1812–1870):** English writer. Dickens is considered the greatest Victorian author. He wrote numerous world classics, such as *A Christmas Carol, David Copperfield, A Tale of Two Cities,* and *Great Expectations,* as well as many works of social criticism.

**Emily Dickinson (1830–1886):** American poet. Dickinson was mostly unknown in her time. She is now considered one of the most important poets in the English language. Together with Walt Whitman, Dickinson is considered the founder of a uniquely American style.

**Annie Dillard (1945– ):** American writer. Dillard is best known for her essays and narrative nonfiction that are lyrical, but difficult to classify due to a very broad range. At age twenty-nine, she won the Pulitzer for her *Pilgrim at Tinker Creek*, about the natural world around her home. She also taught university English for over two decades.

**Fyodor Dostoevsky (1821–1881):** Russian writer. Dostoevsky's novels include *Crime and Punishment* and *The Brothers Karamazov*. He explored psychological complexity in nineteenth-century Russia with a universalist theme. He is considered the founder of the modern existential novel.

**Thomas Dreier (1884–1976):** American editor, writer, business theorist, and philanthropist. Dreier was born on a Wisconsin farm. He founded his own business publication company. During the Great Depression, he retired to a farm where he wrote on the "simple life." Dreier later moved to St. Petersburg, Florida, where he was very active in philanthropic works.

**Eleonora Duse (1858–1924):** Italian actress. Often called simply "Duse," she was known for eschewing makeup and promoting a more naturalistic style; now most famous for her roles in the plays of Gabriele d'Annunzio and Henrik Ibsen.

**Wayne Dyer (1940–2015):** American self-help writer and motivational speaker. Dyer's first book, *Your Erroneous Zones*, was a huge bestseller. His later works reflect more spiritual themes.

**Meister Eckhart (Eckhart von Hochheim) (c. 1260–1327):** German Christian mystic and theologian. Eckhart was a member of the Dominican order. When charged with heresy for his teachings of mystical union with God, he refuted these charges with reasoned arguments. Eckhart had a great influence on later Western mysticism.

**Max Ehrmann (1872–1945):** American attorney and writer. Ehrmann wrote mostly on spiritual themes. His prose poem *Desiderata* became popular and influential after his death.

**Albert Einstein (1879–1955):** German-Swiss-American mathematical physicist. Einstein is one of the greatest theoreticians in physics. He formulated special and general theories of relativity that revolutionized scientific thought. He urged international control for nuclear weapons.

**Duke Ellington (Edward Kennedy Ellington) (1899–1974):** American pianist, composer, and bandleader. Ellington was one of the leading jazz bandleaders, with a longstanding engagement at the Harlem nightspot the Cotton Club. He is famous for such standards as "Sophisticated Lady" and "Mood Indigo."

**Ralph Waldo Emerson (1803–1882):** American poet and essayist. Emerson was the leader of the American transcendentalist philosophical school. He argued for spiritual independence, intuition, and individualism.

**Nora Ephron (1941–2012):** American journalist and writer. Ephron is best known for her hit film screenplays *Silkwood, When Harry Met Sally...,* and *Sleepless in Seattle.*

**Epictetus (c. 55–135 c.e.):** Greco-Roman philosopher. Epictetus was a former slave, and later became one of the most influential Stoic philosophers. He argued that fate controls our lives, and we must accept its vicissitudes calmly and dispassionately.

**Walter Farley (1915–1989):** American writer. Farley is best known for his horse stories, particularly the classic *The Black Stallion.*

**F. Scott Fitzgerald (1896–1940):** American writer. Fitzgerald is known for his novels and short stories, particularly about the so-called "Lost Generation" of young people after the First World War. He is widely regarded as one of the greatest American writers, particularly for his classic, *The Great Gatsby*.

**Cotton Fitzsimmons (1931–2004):** American basketball coach. Fitzsimmons led the NBA team the Phoenix Suns and other teams to championship seasons. He was named NBA Coach of the Year twice.

**Michael J. Fox (1961– ):** Canadian American actor and activist. Fox has a prominent film and acting career, notably as Marty McFly in the Back to the Future series. He was diagnosed with Parkinson's disease in 1992 and has since become a prominent activist seeking a cure.

**Anne Frank (1929–1945):** German Jewish diarist and writer. Frank is best known for her diary account of hiding from the Nazis in Amsterdam. She was eventually captured and died in a Nazi concentration camp. Posthumously, her work has been translated into sixty-seven languages and countless stage and screen adaptations.

**Stephen Fry (1957– ):** English comedian, actor, and writer. Fry began his career at Cambridge University, where he joined the Cambridge Footlights comedy troupe, which included Hugh Laurie, Robbie Coltrane, and Emma Thompson. Fry starred as Jeeves on television, and is known for his numerous film roles, novels, and comedy sketches.

**Robert Fulghum (1937– ):** American writer. Fulghum's many previous careers and jobs ranged from ditch digger to Unitarian Universalist minister. He is best known for his huge bestseller, *All I Really Need to Know I Learned in Kindergarten*.

**Neil Gaiman (1960– ):** English author. Gaiman's broad range of works include short stories, graphic novels, and screenplays. His most famous work is his Sandman series, the first comic book to ever win a literary award.

**André Gide (1869–1951):** French writer. Gide wrote fiction as well as an autobiography. His works exhibit the tension between his strict

Protestant upbringing and morality and a desire to overcome social constraints. He was a pioneer in exploring gay themes. Gide won the Nobel Prize in Literature in 1947.

**Elizabeth Gilbert (1969– ):** American writer. Gilbert is best known for her memoir, *Eat, Pray, Love,* about her world travel and spiritual quest.

**Jack Gilbert (1925–2012):** American poet. Gilbert lived in isolation, but his work, according to the Pulitzer Prize Committee, illuminated "everyday experience with startling clarity."

**Rumer Godden (1907–1998):** English writer. Godden was the acclaimed and prolific author of over sixty fiction and nonfiction works. Her novels set in India have been praised for their atmosphere.

**Johann Wolfgang von Goethe (1749–1832):** German writer, scientist, and court official. His tumultuous early life of passionate love affairs was reflected in his writing; this made him the darling of the poets of the Romantic movement. In his later years, a more sedate Goethe completed his masterpiece, *Faust,* about a man who makes a pact with the devil.

**Elizabeth Goudge (1900–1984):** English writer. Goudge is known for her novels, short stories, and children's books, all of which are infused with spirituality, and which often interweave myth and legend into the plot.

**Martha Graham (1894–1991):** American modern dancer and choreographer. Graham was the founder of the Martha Graham Dance Company, and was a dance innovator. Graham received the Presidential Medal of Freedom in 1976.

**Kenneth Grahame (1859–1932):** Scottish writer. Grahame is best known for his children's classic, *The Wind in the Willows,* which was written after his early retirement from a banking career.

**Vivian Greene:** American artist, writer, entrepreneur. Greene became the first female greeting card manufacturer in the U.S. at age twenty-one. Greene produces the *Kisses* comic strip which is syndicated in twenty-two countries, and writes inspirational books for both children and adults.

**Chris Hadfield (1959– ):** Canadian astronaut and fighter pilot. Hadfield was the first Canadian to walk in space. He is the author of the bestselling *An Astronaut's Guide to Life on Earth.*

**Hafiz (Khwāja Shams-ud-Dīn Muhammad Hāfez-e Shīrāzī) (c. 1325–1389):** Persian poet. Hafiz's mystical, insightful poems are regarded as classics of literature, still frequently read and recited today.

**Woody Harrelson (1961– ):** American actor. Harrelson gained acting fame as the amiable, dimwitted Woody the bartender in the popular television comedy *Cheers.* He had notable roles in major films such as *Natural Born Killers, The Thin Red Line,* and the Hunger Games movies. Harrelson is also prominent as an environmental activist. He lives in a self-sustaining community in Maui, Hawaii, with his wife and three daughters.

**Joanne Harris (1964– ):** British writer. Harris wrote the bestseller *Chocolat,* about a single mother who opens a chocolate shop in a small French village and changes the lives of all those around her.

**Sophie B. Hawkins (1964– ):** American singer, songwriter, and actress. Hawkins's debut album *Tongues and Tails* contained her hit single "Damn I Wish I Was Your Lover." After an artistic battle with Sony Records, she founded her own label, Trumpet Swan Productions.

**Nathaniel Hawthorne (1804–1864):** American writer. Hawthorne is considered one of America's greatest authors. He wrote acclaimed short stories and the classics *The Scarlet Letter* and *The House of the Seven Gables.*

**Robert A. Heinlein (1907–1988):** American writer. Heinlein was called "the dean of science fiction writers." He wrote "hard science" fiction with many scientifically plausible speculations. He was a four-time Hugo winner. His stories also had themes of political freedom and sexual liberation.

**Jim Henson (1936–1990):** American puppeteer and filmmaker. Henson rose to fame when he joined the children's TV show *Sesame Street*, where he developed numerous characters. He made Muppet movies and characters for other films as well.

**Audrey Hepburn (1929–1993):** Belgian-born British actress and humanitarian. Hepburn began her career as a dancer and model until she was spotted by film producers. She won an Academy Award for *Roman Holiday*. She had acclaimed film roles in *Breakfast at Tiffany's, My Fair Lady, Charade,* and numerous others. Hepburn was also an ambassador for the United Nations Children's Fund (UNICEF).

**Hermann Hesse (1877–1962):** German-Swiss writer and painter. Hesse is best known for his mystical novels, which explore human spirituality, especially *Steppenwolf, Siddhartha,* and *The Glass Bead Game (Magister Ludi)*. Hesse received the Nobel Prize in Literature in 1946.

**Marjorie Pay Hinckley (1911–2004):** American writer. Hinckley was the wife of the president of the Church of Jesus Christ of Latter-day Saints (Mormons) and mother of five children. She wrote on the joys of motherhood and the simple things in life.

**Alfred Hitchcock (1899–1980):** English filmmaker. Hitchcock was nicknamed the "Master of Suspense" for his numerous thrillers, often with a distinctive element of humor. He directed such classics as *The 39 Steps, Rear Window, North by Northwest,* and *Psycho*.

**David Hockney (1937– ):** British artist. A major figure in the Pop Art movement, Hockney is best known for his photo collages and famous paintings of Los Angeles swimming pools. He is considered one of Britain's most influential artists.

. . . . . . . . . . . . . . . . . . . . . . . . . . . . . . . . . . . . . . . . . . . . . . . . . . . . . . . . . . . . . . . . . . . . .

"NOTHING IS WORTH MORE...

**Edward Hopper (1882–1967)**: American artist. Hopper was called the "quintessential realist painter of twentieth-century America." He painted everyday scenes of motel rooms, cafeterias, and street scenes, often investing them with a poignant sense of loneliness and alienation.

**Nick Hornby (1957– )**: British writer. Hornby is best known for *Fever Pitch*, his autobiographical account of his fanatical fanhood for Arsenal, the football club, and also for his bestselling and award-winning novels *High Fidelity* and *About a Boy*.

**James Howe (1946– )**: American writer of children's and young adult books. Howe is best known for his series about a vampire rabbit, Bunnicula, created with his then-wife Deborah. He has gone on to write other children's books, young adult novels, screenplays, and more.

**Irene Hunt (1907–2001)**: American writer. Hunt is best known for her children's historical fiction, including *Across Five Aprils*, and *Up a Road Slowly*, which won the Newbery Medal.

**Robert Green Ingersoll (1833–1899)**: American lawyer, politician, and prominent advocate of agnosticism. Ingersoll was considered the greatest orator of his time in the U.S.

**Molly Ivins (1944–2007)**: American journalist. Her column was syndicated to 400 newspapers, with a liberal populist viewpoint.

**A. J. Jacobs (1968– )**: American journalist and writer. Jacobs practices a style of journalism called immersion or "stunt journalism." He immerses himself in a project—such as reading the entire *Encyclopedia Britannica*—and then writes about it.

**Quincy Jones (1933– )**: American record producer, arranger, and composer. Originally Jones was the trumpet player for Lionel Hampton. He arranged songs for such greats as Count Basie. He was the musical director for Dizzy Gillespie and later for

Mercury Records. Jones wrote numerous film scores for such movies as *The Color Purple*. He also produced many Michael Jackson hits, including *Thriller*.

**Michael Jordan (1963– ):** American basketball player. Jordan is considered by many to be the greatest basketball player of all time. He is the winner of five MVP awards, ten All-NBA First Team designations, and nine All-Defensive First Team honors. Jordan is also known as one of the most successful sports marketers and promoters.

**Jon Kabat-Zinn (1944– ):** American professor and medical scientist. Kabat-Zinn is known for his integration of Eastern yogic and Buddhist teachings into a Western "mindfulness" meditation practice for stress reduction. His programs are offered by numerous medical centers throughout the world.

**Frida Kahlo (1907–1954):** Mexican painter. Kahlo combined Mexican and Amerindian themes in her painting. She is best known for her self-portraits.

**Wassily Kandinsky (1866–1944):** Russian artist and art theorist. Kandinsky was a leader in the abstract art movement, and is considered the first painter to produce purely abstract works. He had the gift of synesthesia, i.e., he could hear colors and see sounds.

**Immanuel Kant (1724–1804):** German philosopher. Kant was one of the most influential figures of modern philosophy. Much of his work centered on the question: What can we know? His *Critique of Pure Reason* defined the limits and scope of reason.

**Helen Keller (1880–1968):** American writer and lecturer. Keller became blind and deaf after an illness at nineteen months. Despite her disabilities, she became a political activist, lectured extensively, and wrote numerous books, including *The Story of My Life*. She received the Presidential Medal of Freedom in 1964.

**Gene Kelly (1912–1996):** American dancer, actor, choreographer, and film producer. Kelly is best known for his athletic dancing style and roles in such musical film classics as *Singin' in the Rain* and *An American in Paris.*

**Corita Kent (1918–1986):** American artist and educator. Originally a nun, Kent was credited with transforming silkscreen printing into a fine art medium. Her designs were usually colorful with messages of hope and peace, such as her famous 1985 "Love" U.S. postage stamp.

**Jack Kerouac (1922–1969):** American writer. Kerouac was a pioneering member of the Beat Generation, known for his method of spontaneous prose. After years of rejection, his autobiographical work about his travels, *On the Road,* became a huge success. Other writings deal with Buddhism, spiritual issues, jazz, drugs, and travel.

**Alicia Keys (stage name of Alicia Augello Cook) (1980– ):** American musician. Keys is best known as an R&B singer/songwriter. Her debut album, *Songs in A Minor,* sold over twelve million copies. She has won five Grammys so far.

**Vilayat Inayat Khan (1916–2004):** Sufi meditation master and teacher. Khan was born in London, studied cello as a youth, and served in the Royal Navy during World War II. Later, following in the footsteps of his father (who was the founder of the Sufi Order in the West), Khan taught Universal Sufism—that all religions are as rays of light from the same sun. Throughout his life he was active in multifaith movements.

**Omar Khayyam (or Umar Khayyam) (c. 1048–1131):** Persian poet, mathematician, and astronomer. He was known primarily in the East for his scientific accomplishments. In the West, he is best known for his *rubaiyat,* or quatrains, which were translated by Edward FitzGerald.

**Stephen King (1947– ):** American writer. King is known as the quintessential American horror author with total book sales of over half a billion copies and numerous films made of such classics as *Carrie*, *The Stand*, and *The Shining*.

**Rudyard Kipling (1865–1936):** English writer. Kipling was one of the most popular authors of both poetry and prose of his era. His children's books, notably *Kim*, and his poetry, especially of soldier life in British India, are considered classics, although his pro-imperial attitudes have subjected his writing to much criticism as well.

**E. L. (Elaine Lobl) Konigsburg (1930–2013):** American writer and illustrator, especially of children's books. Konigsburg is the author of the children's classic *From the Mixed-Up Files of Mrs. Basil E. Frankweiler*. She is the winner of two Newbery medals.

**Dean Koontz (1945– ):** American writer. Koontz is best known for his bestselling thrillers which often contain elements of science fiction and horror. He reportedly spends over seventy hours a week writing, and has been published under several different pseudonyms. He has also created several graphic novel series.

**Besa Kosova:** Albanian-born American writer and literacy advocate. Kosova is the author of a collection of poems, *Raindrops*.

**Jiddu Krishnamurti (1895–1986):** Indian-born philosophical and spiritual leader. He shunned national and religious labels, and stressed the need for individual change in the psyche, brought about by intense personal reflection.

**Kris Kristofferson (1936– ):** American musician, singer, and actor. Kristofferson is best known for composing the hit "Me and Bobby McGee" and many other popular songs as well as numerous film roles.

**Stanley Kunitz (1905–2006):** American poet. Kunitz was appointed Poet Laureate of the United States in 1974 and in 2000. He is known for his symbolic poetry with echoes of Carl Jung. He was also a passionate gardener.

**Harold Kushner** (1935– ): American religious leader. Kushner is a rabbi of the progressive wing of Conservative Judaism. He is known for his bestselling book about the problem of evil, *When Bad Things Happen to Good People.*

**Wally Lamb** (1950– ): American writer. Lamb is best known for his acclaimed and bestselling novels, *She's Come Undone* and *I Know This Much Is True.* He also has taught creative writing for many years, and is active in a writing program for incarcerated women.

**Anne Lamott** (1954– ): American writer. Lamott is best known for her nonfiction semi-autobiographical works.

**Jake LaMotta** (1921– ): American boxer. LaMotta was nicknamed the "Bronx Bull" and the "Raging Bull." He is a former World Middleweight Champion. His autobiography, *Raging Bull: My Story,* inspired the classic Academy Award–winning film by Martin Scorsese.

**D. H. (David Herbert) Lawrence** (1885–1930): English writer. A prolific writer, Lawrence began as a poet who often evoked the natural world. His novels, most famously *Lady Chatterley's Lover,* often controversially explored sexual themes and the dehumanizing effects of modern industrialized society.

**Cloris Leachman** (1926– ): American actress. Leachman is the winner of nine Emmy Awards, best known for her role as the overbearing landlady in the hit television series *The Mary Tyler Moore Show.*

**Harper Lee** (1926– ): American writer. Lee is the author of the classic novel *To Kill a Mockingbird,* which dealt with racism in the South. She was the winner of the Presidential Medal of Freedom in 2007.

**John Lennon** (1940–1980): English musician and songwriter. Lennon is known internationally as a founder of the rock group the Beatles. Together with fellow Beatles, especially Paul McCartney, he wrote and performed some of the most successful songs of the twentieth century.

C. S. (Clive Staples) Lewis (1898–1963): Irish-born British writer. Lewis was a Christian apologist and Cambridge professor. He is celebrated both for his scholarly works on medieval literature and his Christian works for adults (*The Screwtape Letters*, etc.) and children (*The Chronicles of Narnia*).

Martin Luther (1483–1546): German theologian. Luther was a major church reformer. He instigated the Protestant Reformation in Germany and neighboring countries.

David Lynch (1946– ): American filmmaker of surrealistic popular films and television. Lynch is the creator of the alternative film *Eraserhead* and the hit TV series *Twin Peaks*.

J. Lynn (pseudonym of Jennifer L. Armentrout) (1980– ): American writer. Under the J. Lynn name, she writes adult romance, but she is best known for her bestselling young adult novels under her real name.

Agnes Martin (1912–2004): American artist. Martin did chiefly abstract expressionist or minimalist painting, often centered around Eastern philosophical themes. She was awarded a National Medal of Arts in 1998.

Groucho Marx (Julius Henry Marx) (1890–1977): American comedian. He was the wisecracking member of the famed comedy team the Marx Brothers. Marx cowrote a series of famous screenplays, and later hosted a TV show. He also wrote his autobiography as well as a serious study of the income tax.

A. H. (Abraham Harold) Maslow (1908–1970): American psychologist. Maslow is known for his theory of the individual's hierarchy of needs, which culminates in a high state of psychological being he termed "self-actualization."

**William Matthews (1942–1997):** American poet and essayist. Matthews was praised for his "personal voice." He won the National Book Critics Circle Award for his poetry. He also taught English and creative writing at various universities.

**Henri Matisse (1869–1954):** French artist. Matisse, along with Picasso, was an extremely important innovator in modern art. His work as a Fauvist emphasized bright, vibrant colors.

**W. S. (William Somerset) Maugham (1874–1965):** British writer. Maugham is best known for his short stories and autobiographical novel *Of Human Bondage.* He led an adventurous life, and served in the British secret service in both World Wars I and II.

**Nikki McClure (1968– ):** American artist. McClure is based in Olympia, Washington. She specializes in intricate paper-cut art, often with a nature-based theme.

**Henry Miller (1891–1980):** American writer. Miller is famous for his Bohemian semi-autobiographical novels, particularly *Tropic of Cancer, The Colossus of Maroussi,* and *Tropic of Capricorn.* After living in Europe, he eventually settled in Big Sur, California.

**Debbie Millman:** American graphic designer, brand consultant, writer, and educator. She is the host of the podcast Design Matters. Her work is characterized by hand-drawn typography.

**A. A. (Alan Alexander) Milne (1882–1956):** English writer. Milne is famed for his childhood classic *Winnie-the-Pooh* and his children's verse.

**Joan Miró (1893–1983):** Catalan Spanish artist. Miró is famed for his surrealistic style and work in painting, ceramics, and sculpture. He greatly influenced American abstract expressionists; masterpieces include the large ceramic murals *Wall of the Moon* and *Wall of the Sun* in Paris.

**Helen Mirren (1945– ):** British actress. Mirren is a winner of multiple acting awards, including an Academy Award, a Tony Award, three Golden Globes, and four Emmy Awards. She received a damehood from Queen Elizabeth in 2003.

**Claude Monet (1840–1926):** French artist. Monet was a founder of the French Impressionist style of painting, which captured light and natural forms. He is widely seen as one of the world's greatest artists.

**Ashley Montagu (1905–1999):** British-born American anthropologist. He is known for his strident opposition to the validity of race as a biological concept, for which he was dismissed from his professorship at Rutgers University. He retired to write on mother-infant relations.

**Michel Eyquem de Montaigne (1533–1592):** French writer. Montaigne was a pioneer of the essay (his own word for what he wrote) in Renaissance Europe. He was a philosophical thinker who sought by means of writing his *essais*, or trials, to stylistically address diverse topics in a format with ideas and mixed with anecdotes and digressions.

**L. M. (Lucy Maud) Montgomery (1874–1942):** Canadian writer. Her first novel, *Anne of Green Gables*, about a red-haired orphan on Prince Edward Island, was an immediate international bestseller. Montgomery went on to write numerous sequels.

**Joye Moon:** American artist. She is best known for her watercolors. Moon is also a writer on art and gives seminars on painting.

**Toni Morrison (nee Chloe Ardelia Wofford)(1931– ):** American writer, novelist, memoirist. Morrison is known for capturing the African American experience and voice. She is the recipient of a Pulitzer Prize and the first African American to receive a Nobel Prize in Literature (1993).

**John Muir (1838–1914):** Scottish-born American naturalist and writer. Muir wrote numerous vivid letters, essays, and books particularly on the Sierra Nevada mountains. He was also a talented inventor and explorer. For a while he lived in a small cabin in Yosemite Valley. His activism helped put Yosemite and the great sequoia woods under the National Park System.

**Iris Murdoch (1919–1999):** Irish-born British writer. Murdoch is considered one of the most influential English writers of the twentieth century. Her works focus on finding meaning in life. She is the winner of the Booker Prize for *The Sea, the Sea.*

**Lauren Myracle (1969– ):** American writer, mostly of young adult fiction. She is best known for her three bestselling IM novels, *ttyl*, *ttfn*, and *l8r, g8r*, and for the controversies surrounding her inclusion of alcohol and homosexuality in her books.

**Vladimir Nabokov (1899–1977):** Russian-born American writer. His early works are in Russian. He is best known for his *Lolita*, consistently ranked as among the best American novels. He also worked as a translator, professor, chess theorist, and lepidopterist.

**Vera Nazarian (1966– ):** Armenian Russian–born American writer of science fiction and fantasy "wonder" supernatural novels. She often combines myth with her ethnic background in her work.

**Cynthia Nelms (Nelms-Byrne):** American artist. Nelms was originally a mortgage banker. After years spent in Colorado and California and studying art in Spain, she settled in Iowa, where she ran a gallery. She now focuses on painting and commercial art.

**Willie Nelson (1933– ):** American singer/songwriter. Nelson is a Texas-born country music star, with an iconic style that has ranged from reggae, blues, jazz, and folk. He is also an activist and environmentalist.

**Petra Němcová (1979– ):** Czech model, television host, and philanthropist. Němcová's appearance in the *Sports Illustrated* swimsuit issue broke her into supermodel status. She became a humanitarian after surviving the 2004 Indian Ocean tsunami.

**Bob Newhart (1929– ):** American comedian and actor. Newhart achieved fame doing deadpan monologues. He was later the star of two hit television series.

**Jack Nicholson (1937– ):** American actor. Nicholson is a screen icon, beginning with his breakthrough role in the countercultural classic *Easy Rider;* seminal roles include *Five Easy Pieces, Chinatown, One Flew Over the Cuckoo's Nest,* and *Terms of Endearment.* He has won numerous awards, including three Academy Awards.

**Shauna Niequist:** American writer. Niequist focuses on food, family, and everyday life with spirtual elements.

**Friedrich Nietzsche (1844–1900):** German philosopher and philologist. Nietzsche's work focused on religion, morality, contemporary culture, philosophy, and science. He promulgated the concepts of the Will to Power, the death of God, nihilism, and the Übermensch (superman).

**Anaïs Nin (1903–1977):** Spanish-Cuban-French writer. Nin lived most of her life in the U.S. A prolific author, she was acclaimed for her deeply self-exploratory journals and her female erotica. Her journals and *Delta of Venus* are considered classics.

**Henri J. M. Nouwen (1932–1996):** Dutch-born Catholic priest. Nouwen was a professor of theology. He worked with the intellectually disabled at the L'Arche Daybreak community in Richmond Hill, Ontario. His influential writings centered on his problems with depression and his struggle to reconcile faith and celibacy with the need for love and intimacy.

**Seán O'Casey (1880–1964):** Irish playwright. O'Casey was born in a poor section of Dublin. He worked as a laborer before becoming a playwright. His first plays dealt with the life of the poor and his later plays were more experimental and impressionistic.

**Georgia O'Keeffe (1887–1986):** American artist. Best known for her portrayal of the essential abstract forms in nature, especially landscapes, bones, and flowers; her budlike erotic flowers are particularly famous.

**Eugene O'Neill (1888–1953):** Irish American playwright. O'Neill was the winner of the Nobel Prize in Literature in 1936. His mostly tragic plays of everyday Americans introduced realism into American theater.

**Chuck Palahniuk (1962– ):** American writer. He is best known for his breakout novel *Fight Club*, which was published after initial rejections of other works, and a peripatetic career as a journalist, technical writer, and diesel mechanic.

**Grace Paley (1922–2007):** American writer. Paley is best known for her widely anthologized short fiction. She also wrote poetry and taught creative writing. She was a prominent peace activist.

**Robert (Bob) Parsons (1950– ):** American entrepreneur. Parsons was born to a poor family in inner city Baltimore. He graduated magna cum laude from the University of Baltimore. As a self-taught programmer, he founded an accounting technology company and became a billionaire.

**Dan Pearce (1978– ):** American blogger, artist, and writer. He is best known for his blog *Single Dad*.

**Tyler Perry (1969– ):** American actor, director, screenwriter, and playwright. Many of his works have strong moral and Christian themes.

**Pablo Picasso (1881–1973):** Spanish painter and sculptor. He is famed for his artistic innovation and versatility as well as for the beauty of his creations. *Guernica* is one of his Cubist masterpieces, a style he pioneered.

**Christopher Pike (pseudonym of Kevin Christopher McFadden) (1954– ):** American author. Pike is the bestselling writer of teen thrillers.

**Jackson Pollock (1912–1956):** American artist. Pollock was a major figure in the Abstract Expressionist movement and an innovator of the drip-painting style.

**Terry Pratchett (1948–2015):** English writer of fantasy and science fiction novels. He is the author of the famous Discworld series about events on a flat world balanced on the back of four elephants. He has sold over 85 million books worldwide.

**Jacques Prévert (1900–1977):** French poet and screenwriter. Prévert was considered a leading Surrealist poet. He worked at reviving the ancient style of oral poetry. His anti-clerical, anarchistic, iconoclastic, and humorous poems were immensely popular. He was also a top screenwriter in the 1930s and '40s.

**Marcel Proust (1871–1922):** French writer. He is best known for his long and immensely detailed semi-autobiographical stream-of-consciousness novel, *À la recherche du temps perdu* (*Remembrance of Things Past*), considered a classic of world literature.

**Ptolemy (Claudius Ptolemy) (c. 90–168 c.e.):** Greco Egyptian scientist. His astronomical and geographical works formed the basis of medieval Western and Arab sciences.

**Edward M. Purcell (1912–1997):** American physicist. He won the Nobel Prize in 1952 for his discovery of nuclear magnetic resonance in liquids and in solids. He was also famous for his pioneering and innovative introductory text *Electricity and Magnetism,* which used Einstein's relativity theory at an elementary level.

**Anna Quindlen (1952– ):** American journalist and writer. She won the Pulitzer Prize for her *New York Times* column in 1992. She went on to write bestselling novels and commentary.

**Julia Quinn (pseudonym of Julie Pottinger, born Julie Cotler) (1970– ):** American writer. Quinn is best known for her bestselling historical romances. She first wrote novels in medical school, but was so successful she left her studies to write full time.

**Gilda Radner (1946–1989):** American comedian and actress. She was an original cast member of the hit comedy series *Saturday Night Live* and is known for her hilarious characters, such as the hard-of-hearing Emily Litella.

**Robert Redford (1936– ):** American actor, producer, director, and activist. As a major film star with a handsome all-American look, he was noted for roles in such acclaimed films as *Butch Cassidy and the Sundance Kid* and *The Sting*. He directed many award-winning movies, such as *A River Runs Through It*, and is a founder of the Sundance Film Festival, which highlights independent films and documentaries.

**Keith Richards (1943– ):** English rock musician. He was an original member of the group the Rolling Stones. With Mick Jagger, he wrote such classic hits as "Jumpin' Jack Flash," acclaimed by *Rolling Stone* magazine for "rock's greatest single body of riffs on guitar."

**Nora Roberts (1950– ):** American writer. She is best known for her romance novels and has written over 209 works.

**Fred Rogers (known as Mister Rogers) (1928–2003):** American educator and minister. Rogers is best known as the television host of the popular and gentle children's TV morning show *Mister Rogers' Neighborhood*, winner of four Emmy Awards.

**Will Rogers (1879–1935):** American humorist and performer. Rogers is known for his "down home" social commentary. He became the top paid Hollywood star in the mid-1930s. He was killed during an around-the-world airplane trip with aviator Wiley Post.

**Andy Rooney (1919–2011):** Journalist and news commentator. He won celebrity as the irascible, curmudgeonly commentator on life's foibles on television's *60 Minutes.*

**Eleanor Roosevelt (1884–1962):** American humanitarian and writer. As First Lady, she advised her husband, President Franklin Delano Roosevelt, in political and social affairs, serving as assistant director of civilian defense. Later she worked as a delegate to the UN Assembly and was chairperson of the UN Human Rights Commission. She is known worldwide for her tireless advocacy of humanitarian causes.

**Arthur Rubinstein (1888–1982):** Polish-born American pianist. Rubinstein studied with Ignacy Jan Paderewski. He toured Europe as a virtuoso in the early 1900s. After World War II, he lived in the U.S. and made extensive worldwide concert tours.

**Rumi (Jalil al-Din) (1207–1273):** Sufi poet. Rumi was one of the most influential Sufi writers/leaders. He is known for his mystic verses, and founded the Mevlevi order. His mystic poems, originally written in Persian, have been translated into numerous languages. Rumi was declared America's most popular poet in 2007.

**Carl Sandburg (1878–1967):** American writer. He was a Pulitzer Prize–winning poet and a biographer of Abraham Lincoln. He was called the "quintessentially American writer."

**William Saroyan (1908–1981):** American writer. He won the Pulitzer Prize for Drama in 1940, and an Academy Award in 1943 for the story turned into a film, *Human Comedy.* His works focused on Armenian immigrant life in California.

**May Sarton (1912–1995):** Belgian-born American writer. She is best known for her memoirs dealing with issues of a solitary life. Although she wrote of her lesbianism, she wanted to be appreciated for her writing on the universal human condition.

**Mary Schmich (1953– ):** American writer and journalist. She is a columnist for *The Chicago Tribune* and writer of the famous *Brenda Starr* comic for twenty-eight years.

**Louie Schwartzberg (1950– ):** American filmmaker. He is a pioneer of time-lapse cinematography.

**Albert Schweitzer (1875–1965):** Alsatian missionary, theologian, musician, and philosopher. He founded and built a hospital in what was then French Equatorial Africa. He was awarded the Nobel Peace Prize in 1952 for his "reverence for life" philosophy.

**Jo Scott-B:** Argentine-born Canadian artist, painter, and illustrator. She is active in local British Columbian artistic and civic circles.

**Jerry Seinfeld (1954– ):** American comedian and actor. Seinfeld has a unique style of observational humor. His eponymous television series was a huge hit.

**Dr. Seuss (pseudonym of Theodor Geisel) (1904–1991):** American writer and illustrator. Dr. Seuss created numerous children's classics, such as *The Cat in the Hat, Green Eggs and Ham,* and *How the Grinch Stole Christmas,* with catchy rhymes and characteristic humorous illustrations. His books have has over 200 million copies in print.

**William Shakespeare (1564–1616):** English playwright and poet. He was called "the Bard of Avon." He is widely considered the English-speaking world's leading dramatist. His plays have been performed more than those of any other writer.

**Paul Simon (1941– ):** American musician. He is best known as the singer/songwriter of the Simon & Garfunkel duo, with such hits as "The Sound of Silence." He went on to a very successful solo career. He is the winner of twelve Grammy Awards.

**Betty Smith (1896–1972):** American writer. Her famous first novel, *A Tree Grows in Brooklyn,* based on her own experience growing up in poverty in Williamsburg, Brooklyn, celebrates tenacity and initiative.

**Logan Pearsall Smith (1865–1946):** American-born writer. He lived much of his life in England. He produced critical editions of various authors, and is best known for his short stories and essays.

**Aleksandr Solzhenitsyn (1918–2008):** Russian writer. He was a stern critic of the Soviet Union. He wrote *The Gulag Archipelago, One Day in the Life of Ivan Denisovich,* and *Cancer Ward,* which focused on communist repression and the prison camp system. He was awarded the Nobel Prize in Literature in 1970.

**Nicholas Sparks (1965– ):** American writer. Sparks is best known for his international bestseller *The Notebook.* It was picked out of a slush pile by an agent, and went on to receive a one-million-dollar advance and eventually become a bestseller. Sparks went on to write more bestsellers, which have also been made into films.

**Gertrude Stein (1874–1946):** American writer and critic. She influenced contemporary artists and applied theories of abstract art to writing. She maintained an unofficial salon for American expatriate writers and artists like Ernest Hemingway and F. Scott Fitzgerald at her Left Bank Paris apartment.

**Emma Stone (1988– ):** American actress. Her film debut was in *Superbad* in 2007, and she has gone on to star in many hit movies. She was nominated for an Academy Award in 2015 for her role in *Birdman: Or (The Unexpected Virtue of Ignorance).*

**Tom Stoppard (1937– ):** British playwright, born in Zlín, Czechoslovakia (now the Czech Republic), as Tomas Straussler. As a child, Stoppard and his family fled Nazi persecution, and after early schooling in Darjeeling, India, settled in England. There he started as a journalist, then became an acclaimed playwright whose plays combine wit with profound philosophical insight. He was knighted in 1997.

**Donald Sutherland (1935– ):** Canadian actor. His acting career spans almost fifty years, with numerous notable and diverse roles in films ranging from the classic *M\*A\*S\*H* to *The Hunger Games.*

**Rabindranath Tagore (1861–1941):** Indian poet, novelist, and philosopher. He founded a school seeking to blend Eastern and Western philosophies and educational systems. His poetry reflects this blending. He won the Nobel Prize in Literature in 1913.

**Thích Nhất Hạnh (1926– ):** Vietnamese Zen Buddhist monk. He is currently residing in the Plum Village Monastery in the south of France. He writes and gives retreats and lectures worldwide on nonviolence and mindfulness meditation.

**Hunter S. Thompson (1937–2005):** American journalist. He created a writer-participatory, stylized form of journalism, which he called Gonzo journalism. He is also known for his wild lifestyle and celebration of heavy drinking, psychedelic drugs, and firearms.

**Henry David Thoreau (1817–1852):** American naturalist, writer, activist, and transcendentalist. He is best known for his philosophy of civil disobedience—elucidated in his essay "Civil Disobedience" as well as his famous book *Walden,* about his solitary life at Walden Pond.

**J.R.R. (John Ronald Reuel) Tolkien (1892–1973):** English writer and scholar. Tolkien was an Oxford philologist of Anglo-Saxon literature. He is best known for his classic fantasy novels *The Hobbit* and *The Lord of the Rings* trilogy.

**Leo Tolstoy (1828–1910):** Russian writer and moralist. Tolstoy was a pioneer of the "psychological novel." His most famous masterpieces were *War and Peace* and *Anna Karenina*. He fought in the Crimean War, which inspired his anti-war attitudes. Toward the end of his life, he turned over his fortune to his wife and lived as a peasant.

**Desmond Tutu (1931– ):** South African clergyman and activist. Tutu is one of the most prominent anti-apartheid activists. He was awarded the Nobel Peace Prize in 1984, the Albert Schweitzer Prize for Humanitarianism in 1986, the Gandhi Peace Prize in 2007, and the Presidential Medal of Freedom in 2009.

**Mark Twain (pseudonym of Samuel Langhorne Clemens) (1835–1910):** American writer. Twain is best known for the classics *The Adventures of Tom Sawyer* and *The Adventures of Huckleberry Finn*, accounts drawn from his own boyhood. He was the preeminent American humorist and satirist of the nineteenth century.

**Neil deGrasse Tyson (1958– ):** American astrophysicist. He is the director of New York's Hayden Planetarium and research associate in astrophysics at the American Museum of Natural History. He is well known for his hosting of public television science shows.

**John Updike (1932–2009):** American writer. His Rabbit series of novels, for which he won two Pulitzer Prizes, described small-town American Protestant middle-class life.

**Kurt Vonnegut (1922–2007):** American writer. *The New York Times* called Vonnegut the "counterculture's novelist." He wrote numerous bestselling and critically acclaimed novels, which blended satire, science fiction, and humor.

**Alice Walker (1944– ):** American novelist and poet. Walker was influenced by Southern speech patterns and the tradition of storytelling. She was a winner of the National Book Award and Pulitzer Prize for *The Color Purple* (1982).

. . . . . . . . . . . . . . . . . . . . . . . . . . . . . . . . . . . . . . . . . . . . . . . . . . . . . . . . . . . . . . . . . . . . . . . . . . . .

" N O T H I N G   I S   W O R T H   M O R E . . .

**Jo Walton (1964– ):** Welsh Canadian writer of science fiction and fantasy. Many of her works are based on Arthurian legend as well as alternate history. She is a winner of the Nebula and Hugo awards.

**Andy Warhol (1928–1987):** American artist. He was a major influence in the Pop Art movement, which included images from popular culture in artistic creations. His studio, called the Factory, was an important gathering place for intellectuals and artists.

**Bill Watterson (1958– ):** American cartoonist. His classic *Calvin and Hobbes* comic strip is about an iconoclastic little boy and his stuffed tiger. It ran from 1985 to 1995, after which Watterson stopped, saying he felt he had said all there was to say. He is also well known for refusing to license his characters, feeling it would cheapen them.

**Irvine Welsh (1958– ):** Scottish writer. Welsh is best known for his novel *Trainspotting*, which was written in a Scots dialect and shows the underside of Edinburgh life.

**Mae West (1892–1980):** American actress, playwright, and screenwriter. West began in burlesque and vaudeville. She is best known for her film roles (in which she wrote or cowrote her dialogue) marked by witty sexual double entendres.

**Morris L. West (1916–1999):** Australian writer. His novels focus on international politics and the role of the Catholic Church.

**Edith Wharton (1862–1937):** American writer. Wharton is best known for her psychologically insightful novels of America's upper classes. Her novel *The Age of Innocence* won the Pulitzer Prize.

**Joss Whedon (1964– ):** American screenwriter and comic book author. Whedon is best known as the creator of the popular and critically acclaimed TV series *Buffy the Vampire Slayer*. He also created a spin-off show called *Angel*.

**E. B. (Elwyn Brooks) White (1899–1985):** American writer. White is especially known for his classic children's works *Charlotte's Web* and *Stuart Little.* He was also acclaimed for his contributions to *The New Yorker* magazine, most notably his essays and "Notes and Comments."

**Walt Whitman (1819–1892):** American poet. Whitman is known as the father of "free verse." His *Leaves of Grass* is a classic of American literature.

**Laura Ingalls Wilder (1867–1957):** American writer. She is best known for her children's Little House series about pioneer life in the Midwest.

**Thornton Wilder (1897–1975):** American writer and playwright. He won the Pulitzer Prize for his second novel, *The Bridge of San Luis Rey.* He won other Pulitzers for the plays *Our Town* and *The Skin of Our Teeth.* He received the first National Medal for Literature in 1962.

**Marianne Williamson (1952– ):** American writer. She writes mostly on spiritual topics, including four *New York Times* bestsellers.

**Oprah Winfrey (1954– ):** American media mogul and talk-show host. Winfrey was born in poverty in rural Mississippi. She rose to become the world's richest African American. She was the host of the highest-rated talk show in television history, and won numerous Emmy Awards. Winfrey was credited with reviving interest in reading when she featured selected books on her show.

**P. G. (Pelham Grenville) Wodehouse (1881–1975):** English writer. He wrote acclaimed humor novels and short stories, mostly spoofing English gentry.

**Mary Wollstonecraft (1759–1797):** English feminist, writer, and philosopher. Her groundbreaking *A Vindication of the Rights of Woman* argued that women were equal to men and only appeared inferior due to their lack of education. She advocated full rights for women and a social order based on reason.

**Frank Lloyd Wright (1867–1959):** American architect. He is famous for his bold, innovative style that blended with the surrounding environment. His Fallingwater house has been called "the best all-time work of American architecture." He completed the Guggenheim Museum in New York at age ninety-one.

**Christine Wong Yap (1977– ):** American artist. She is best known for her innovative installation art and graphic design.

**W. B. (William Butler) Yeats (1865–1935):** Irish poet. He was the winner of the Nobel Prize in Literature in 1923. He is considered one of the finest of the twentieth-century English-language poets.

**Frank Zappa (1940–1993):** American rock musician and music producer. He produced over sixty albums with his band the Mothers of Invention and as a solo act. He was a leading experimental rocker and social commentator.

# ABOUT THE AUTHORS

Kathryn and Ross Petras, sister-and-brother quotations connoisseurs, have published numerous collections of their finds. Kathryn Petras lives in Seattle; Ross Petras lives in Toronto.

# GIFTS OF WIT AND WISDOM

Hundreds of pithy words, thoughts, and ideas to inspire dreamers and doers.

The best things men and women over 60 have said about how to love, work, laugh, and live.

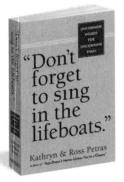

It's tough out there but you're not alone—uncommon wisdom from people who've graduated from the school of hard knocks.

Make a habit of celebrating life, with 618 unexpected rules to live by.